£22·50

# Windows® NT/95 for UNIX Professionals

# Windows® NT/95 for
# UNIX Professionals

**Donald E. Merusi**

***Digital Press***

Boston, Oxford, Johannesburg, Melbourne, New Delhi, Singapore

Digital Press is an imprint of Butterworth–Heinemann.

Copyright © 1997 by Butterworth–Heinemann

 A member of the Reed Elsevier group

Recognizing the importance of preserving what has been written, Butterworth–Heinemann prints its books on acid-free paper whenever possible.

 Butterworth–Heinemann supports the efforts of American Forests and the Global ReLeaf program in its campaign for the betterment of trees, forests, and our environment.

**Library of Congress Cataloging-in-Publication Data**
Merusi, Donald, 1951-
    Windows NT/95 for Unix Professionals / Donald E. Merusi.
        p.   cm.
    Includes index.
    ISBN 1-55558-181-1 (alk. paper)
    Microsoft Windows NT.  2. Microsoft Windows (Computer file)
3. Operating Systems (Computers)   I. Title.
QA76.76.063M465   1997             97-7962
005.4'469--dc21                      CIP

**British Library Cataloguing-in-Publication Data**
A catalogue record for this book is available from the British Library.

The publisher offers special discounts on bulk orders of this book.
For information, please contact:
Manager of Special Sales
Butterworth–Heinemann
313 Washington Street
Newton, MA 02158–1626
Tel: 617-928-2500
Fax: 617-928-2620

For information on all Digital Press publications available, contact our World Wide Web home page at: http://www.bh.com

Order number: EY-W071E-DP

10 9 8 7 6 5 4 3 2 1

Printed in the United States of America

# Contents

# Preface

This book is intended to help users of UNIX systems understand what comparable functionality exists in the Microsoft Windows 95 and Windows NT environments. Specifically, Sun Solaris and the Linux (Slackware version) operating systems are used as the contrast base for UNIX primarily because of their popularity. Topic discussions are hardly exhaustive considering the tremendous scope of the material available and the reader is urged to consult the references listed in Appendix A for more detailed information. Although the book title suggests it is a facility for UNIX professionals to learn Microsoft Windows techniques, it can also work to teach Microsoft Windows professionals UNIX techniques. Many of the discussions presented in the following chapters equitably cover both the UNIX and the Microsoft Windows environments.

**Chapter 1, Introduction to Microsoft Windows and UNIX,** discusses the history and origins of these two operating system environments. Although this chapter presents little technical information, it gives the reader a good perspective on how these two operating system environments evolved into what they are today.

**Chapter 2, The User Interface,** discusses the differences in how users interact with our two operating system environments. The graphical user interface oriented desktops are the focus of discussion in this chapter. The differences between some console command lines are listed in Appendix B. This chapter discusses the differences in how the desktop is used, including desktop object manipulation, desktop characteristics, the file manager, on-line help, the clock, the calculator, mail, and wastebaskets.

**Chapter 3, Building Programs and the Software Management Environment,** discusses the facilities available that help develop, maintain, manage, and preserve software. Discussion focuses on facilities that control and record source code changes, create, compile, build, and debug programs. The Source Code Control System (sccs) is discussed for the UNIX environment. Borland C++ V5.0 is discussed for the Microsoft Windows environment. Backup and archive utilities available in our UNIX and Microsoft Windows environments are also presented.

**Chapter 4, The Win32 API and UNIX System Services**, is a fairly extensive discussion about what system services and APIs are available in our two operating system environments. Topics covered include processes and threads creation and scheduling, performing I/O, memory management, synchronization and concurrency control primitives, and pipes.

**Chapter 5, Networking Facilities**, discusses networking configuration and facilities available in both environments, including TCP/IP, remote procedure calls (RPCs), sockets, PPP and SLIP connections, network file services, and network configuration. The chapter assumes the reader has some familiarity with certain network terms and concepts.

**Chapter 6, System Administration — User Management and Security**, discusses the facilities available in our two operating system environments for maintaining user accounts and system security. This chapter focuses on system-critical files, the Microsoft Windows registry, user groups, user privileges, and printer management.

**Chapter 7, Performance Monitoring**, discusses what facilities exist to monitor the environments of our two operating systems and how they can be used to identify performance bottlenecks. Various monitoring tools are reviewed, including what system-wide metrics can be tracked and what process-specific performance measurement mechanisms exist.

The environments were contrasted as well as they could be with the facilities available to the author. **Appendix A** lists other references for the reader to pursue a more comprehensive discussion about some of the topics discussed in this book. The Internet is an excellent source for discovering computer books. An excellent Web site is Amazon Books at http://www.amazon.com.

**Appendix B** contrasts some commonly performed commands, such as the basic file operations *rename* and *copy*. Both GUI and command-line versions of most of the commands are examined in both the Microsoft Windows and UNIX environments.

**Appendix C** lists commonly performed Windows tasks and how they can be accomplished by using keyboard shortcuts. Sometimes using the keyboard is more expedient than reaching for and manipulating a mouse.

**Appendix D** discusses configuring performance by adjusting settings in the System Properties window from the Control Panel. Hard-drive and CD-ROM caches, video characteristics, and virtual memory settings can be configured from this window.

**Appendix E** discusses how to use the Registry Editor and gives a few examples of the kinds of effects that can be produced by adjusting registry entries.

# Chapter 1

## Introduction to Microsoft Windows and UNIX

This chapter discusses the history, evolution, and system architecture of several of the world's most popular operating systems. The Microsoft Windows environments dominate the world of personal computers, while UNIX is dominant in the world of workstations. This chapter answers the following questions about the history and origins of Microsoft Windows and UNIX:

- Why did Microsoft develop Windows?
- How did Microsoft Windows evolve?
- What features of Windows NT make it different from all previous versions of Windows?
- What is the relationship between Windows NT and Windows 95?
- What is the origin of the UNIX operating system?
- What is Linux?
- What characterizes Sun's Solaris operating system?

## Microsoft Windows — A Short History

The Microsoft Windows environments have their origins in DOS. In 1982, IBM introduced its personal computer and chose command-line-driven DOS as the operating system platform. When Apple released its *graphical user interface* (GUI), Lisa, PC owners were inspired to desire a comparable interface. Using a mouse to point and click was much easier than entering commands. The problem that plagued the development of a GUI for PC owners was one that was to haunt DOS users for years to come—lack of memory. The original machines for which DOS was developed (the Intel 8086 and the Intel 80286) provided limited memory space along with the proverbial 640KB barrier. Not only was memory still a limited resource, Microsoft really was not that interested in developing a GUI for PC owners. It was Digital Research's release of the *Graphical Environment Manager* for the PC that prompted Microsoft to release Version 1.0 of Windows. Versions 1.0 and 2.0 of Windows generated little interest. Version 1.0 was originally called *Interface Manager* and was renamed Microsoft Windows in 1981. Two other versions of Windows were released, Windows/286 and Windows/386. Windows/386 provided the capability to run multiple DOS applications.

In 1987, OS/2 was announced by both Microsoft and IBM as the operating system that would replace DOS. OS/2 has never developed a strong following. Even the latest Warp versions of OS/2 have met with limited success. In 1988, Microsoft hit the jackpot with Windows Version 3.0, and then Version 3.1. This version of Windows had all the right features to make it very attractive to users. Windows for Workgroups (Version 3.11) soon followed, providing networking and multimedia features. Version 3.11 also introduced some 32-bit file system code.

## Windows NT — System Architecture

Windows NT Version 3.1 appeared in 1994 and provided robust system security, interapplication protection, and crash integrity. Microsoft now had an operating system that could provide the kind of soundness required to support a corporate server platform. Windows NT was designed from scratch and is based on the concept of the microkernel. The microkernel design separates all of the operating system functions into independent and distinct subsystems. The kernel performs only very rudimentary functions such as scheduling and communicates with the other subsystems by means of a messaging technology. Microsoft uses *local procedure calls* (LPCs) to accomplish this task. Each subsystem is dedicated to performing a specific task. Some of these subsystems are part of the kernel environment, while some of them actually run as tasks along with user programs! This design makes for a system that is easily extensible and maintainable. Figure 1.1 illustrates the relationship of all the components that are part of a Windows NT environment.

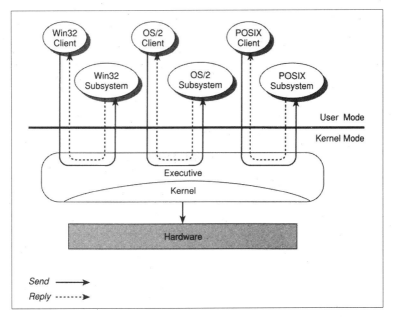

**Figure 1.1.** *Windows NT environment components* (From "Inside Windows NT" by Helen Custer. Reproduced by permission of Microsoft Press. All rights reserved.)

The subsystems that run in user space provide support for interfaces to POSIX, OS/2, the Win32 API and MS-DOS. Theoretically, one can write and install another subsystem to support a completely different interface, such as OpenVMS system services. Running the subsystems in this fashion also provides for improved system integrity. If one of the subsystems should fail, it will abort as another user process and will not compromise the entire system environment.

## Windows NT — Security

Windows NT provides very comprehensive security mechanisms. All users must log in to use the system. At login time, a user is associated with an access token, which acts as a key that defines the kind of access this user has to other objects in the system. All Windows NT objects have a security descriptor associated with them. The security descriptor acts like a lock that the access token key will open to determine what kind of access is possible to the object. Figure 1.2 illustrates the relationships among the security components.

**Figure 1.2.** *Components of Windows NT security*

## Windows NT/95 — True Multitasking

Along with the extensive security environment, Windows NT/95 also provides true multitasking and memory protection between tasks. An NT/95 task can be up to 4GB in size. The elemental scheduling component in Windows NT/95 is the thread. A single process may consist of one or more threads of execution. Threads can be thought of as asynchronously executing subroutines that share a process context. A multithreaded process can have several threads executing simultaneously, each performing a specific task. One thread could be reading data from a disk file, another soliciting input from a user at a terminal, and another performing communication over a network. Threads can be assigned priorities and become involved in a variety of scheduling properties. Threads will be discussed in more detail in Chapter 4.

Thread creation is performed by using the Win32 *Application Program Interface* (API). The Win32 API is an extraordinary collection of functions and routines to perform any systems function imaginable, including process and thread scheduling, concurrency synchronization, memory management, security management, multimedia operations, and much more. We can only discuss a fraction of the overall capability of the Win32 API in this book.

## Windows NT/95 — Networking and the Internet

Networking is an integral part of the Windows NT/95 environment. Windows NT/95 supports many different networking protocols, including TCP/IP, NetBIOS, Appletalk, and IPX. Networking is a transparent part of the user GUI interface. Accessing file folders on remote systems is the same as accessing them locally. From a programming standpoint, Windows NT provides many types of communication interfaces, including *remote procedure calls* (RPCs), sockets, and Windows Network calls.

With the immense popularity of the Internet, browser tools are being packaged with Windows NT. Microsoft's Internet Explorer is installed by default on the NT desktop. NT is also being shipped with Web administration tools, which allows remote server management from any platform with a browser.

## Windows NT/95 — Software Development and Management

A wealth of program development environments are available for Windows NT, because it is one of the hottest operating system platforms in existence today. Many of the programming tools being offered provide the means for designing and implementing Java programs on the Internet. Some of the more notable tools available are Microsoft Visual Basic, Microsoft Visual C/C++, Microsoft Visual J++, Borland C/C++, and Symantec Café. The reader should be aware that Java programs do not run exclusively on the Internet.

## Windows NT Version 4.0

Version 4.0 of Windows NT appeared in the late summer of 1996. This version of NT provides many enhancements over Version 3.51, including some features already available with Windows 95 — such as the same GUI and the ability to maintain very long file names. All Windows NT examples in this book use Version 4.0.

Windows NT Version 4.0 comes in two varieties, server and workstation. The server version is meant to support a large number of departmental clients. The server contains more streamlined networking features and more system administration utilities than the workstation version. NT Server is packaged with an assortment of administrative wizards. Wizards are facilities that walk a user through a particular task. Some of the wizards found in NT can be used to add user accounts, install modems, manage file and folder access, and much more. The NT workstation is the system used on the clients.

## Microsoft Windows NT/95 — The Registry

The registry is a database facility that replaces the the former .INI files and is available in both Windows NT and Windows 95. The registry defines everything in the system:

- Hardware devices
- Device attribute settings
- System environment settings
- Software installed
- Performance data

The user can directly change entries in the registry by calling API routines or by using various registry editors that provide a GUI interface, making it somewhat easier to adjust the resource records. It is somewhat easier because great care must be exercised in manipulating registry entries. All settings must be performed precisely. Any deviation from the prescribed format for a particular resource can result in the system becoming unbootable! Those spirited enough to edit the registry directly are strongly recommended to consult *Windows Resource Kit Handbook*. This manual lists and describes every registry entry.

# Windows 95

Windows 95 (code-named Chicago) appeared in 1995 and provided true 32-bit memory management, true multitasking, long file names, a new GUI interface, and DOS Version 7.0. Although it is similar to Windows NT in many ways, Windows 95 contains none of the system administration or security facilities found in Windows NT. Also, some of the Win32 API calls either are unavailable or perform differently under Windows 95 than under Windows NT. Windows 95 only runs on Intel x86 platforms.

| | |
|---|---|
| **Windows 1.0**<br>1982 • GUI and drop-down menus<br>     • Cooperative multitasking | **Windows for Workgroups V3.1 93-04-22**<br>1992 • First integrated networking package<br>     • Peer-to-peer file/printer sharing<br>     • Introduced Microsoft Mail |
| **Windows 2.0**<br>1987 • Windows that overlap<br>     • PIF files for DOS programs | **Windows for Workgroups 3.1 194-03-01**<br>1994 • 32-bit file system<br>     • Fax<br>     • Improved performance |
| **Windows/386**<br>1987 • Multiple DOS virtual machines with preemptive<br>        multitasking | **Windows 95**<br>1995 • Completely 32-bit<br>     • Full preemptive multitasking<br>     • Includes MS-DOS Version 7.0<br>     • No Windows NT security |
| **Windows 3.0**<br>1990 • Program and File Manager<br>     • Enhanced memory management<br>     • Network support<br>     • More than 16 colors | **Windows NT 3.1 94-03-01**<br>1994 • Architecture supported on Intel x86/Pentium,<br>        MIPS, R4000 Series, and DEC Alpha<br>     • Installable APIs (POSIX, OS/2, etc.)<br>     • Comprehensive security<br>     • Symmetric multiprocessing support |
| **Windows 3.1**<br>1992 • Many improvements to<br>        92-09-21 Version 3.0<br>     • 8086 mode no longer<br>        supported<br>     • *Object Linking and Embedding* (OLE)<br>     • TrueType font support<br>     • Multimedia support<br>     • Improved error diagnostics | • 32-bit addressing (4GB)<br>     • Fully protected applications<br><br>**Windows NT 3.5 94-04-12**<br>1994 • OLE Version 2.0<br>     • Required less memory<br>     • Better performance |
| **Windows 3.1 194-03-01**<br>1992 • Upgrade available free<br>     • Corrects network problems | **Windows NT 4.0 "Cairo" 94-03-15**<br>1995 • Windows 95 GUI |

**Table 1.1.** *Chronology of Microsoft Windows*

## UNIX — A Historical Retrospective

The beginning of UNIX can be traced back to 1969, when Project MAC was being conducted at MIT. The outcome of Project MAC was to be the ultimate operating system, called MULTICS (Multiplexed Operating and Computing System). One of the participating members of Project MAC, Bell Laboratories, did not agree and decided to write their own less complex operating system. The first version of UNIX was written for a PDP-7 by Ken Thompson, who was part of original MULTICS technical staff. Thompson also developed an interpretive language, B, based on BCPL.

Ken Thompson eventually teamed up with Dennis Ritchie, who developed the first C compiler, an improvement on the B language. In 1973, Thompson and Ritchie did what was then considered revolutionary: they rewrote most of UNIX in a high-level language, C. This

| | |
|---|---|
| **Bell Labs Version 1.0**<br>1969    Written for PDP-7 with 4K of 18-bit words | **UTS Version 1.0**<br>1981    Amdahl develops first mainframe version |
| **Bell Labs Version 3.0**<br>1973    Pipes invented | **AT&T System III V1.0**<br>1982    AT&T officially supports UNIX |
| **Bell Labs Version 4.0**<br>1973 • Rewritten in C<br>    • Obtained by University of California<br>    • Berkeley starts to make its enhancements | **SunOS Version 1.0**<br>1982    4.2BSD based on the Motorola 68000 |
| | **ULTRIX V1.0**<br>1982    UNIX from DEC |
| **Version 6.0**<br>1975    First version widely available outside Bell Labs | **AIX Version 1.0**<br>1986    IBM releases its version of UNIX |
| **BSD Version 1.0**<br>1978    Bill Joy produces first Berkeley distribution | **HP/UX Version 1.0**<br>1988    HP releases its version of UNIX |
| **XENIX Version 1.0**<br>1979    Microsoft's version of UNIX for the PC | **SVR4 Version 1.0**<br>1990    Released by UNIX International; unifies BSD, XENIX, and System V |
| **Bell Labs Version 7.0**<br>1979 • Ported to VAX as 32V<br>    • uucp<br>    • Bourne shell<br>    • 40kb kernel | **Solaris Version 1.0**<br>1991    Produced by SunSoft |
| | **BSD Version 4.4**<br>1993    Last release, Berkeley CSRG group disbanded |

**Table 1.2.** *Chronology of UNIX systems*

set the stage for UNIX being ported to any machine platform where it was possible to run the C compiler. In 1974, the first licensed version of UNIX, the Fifth Edition, was produced for the academic community. This caused the proliferation of UNIX to the extent that a multitude of versions were created. Because the source code was distributed, every site customized UNIX to suit its particular needs. The appearance of the Seventh Edition in 1978 began the two distinct paths of UNIX development, SVR4 (AT&T) and BSD (Berkeley Software Distribution). Berkeley enhanced UNIX with some exceptional features, including the C shell, sendmail, TCP/IP support, and virtual memory. Over the years, the features of both SVR4 and BSD have blended together in the current versions of UNIX. Table 1.2 illustrates the UNIX chronology.

## Linux

One of the newest versions of UNIX to appear is Linux, developed by Linus Torvald while he was a student at the University of Helsinki, Finland. Linux is a completely public-domain 32-bit SVR4-flavored version of UNIX. Although written originally for the 386+ class of PCs, it has been ported to virtually every platform. Torvald was inspired by Minix, a student operating system created by computer science professor Andrew Tanebaum. A complete Linux environment can be downloaded directly from the Internet. Three popular packaged forms of Linux are Slackware, Red Hat and Debian. Because Linux is continuously evolving, the reader is urged to consult the appropriate information sources for the latest news about Linux. The Linux organization Web site is an excellent source for the most current information about the Linux distributions. As of the writing of this book, the three Linux distribution packages previously mentioned were available from the Internet at the following locations:

RedHat      ftp.redhat.com/pub
Slackware   ftp.cdrom.com/pub/Linux
Debian      ftp.debian.org

Linux software is archived at the following sites:

```
sunsite.unc.edu
ftp.funet.fi
ftp.cc.gatech.edu
```

Linux is discussed throughout this book as one of the two UNIX environments (the other being Solaris). The Red Hat distribution contains more X-window-based utilities, whereas Slackware and Debian tend to be more text-oriented. This book will use the Slackware version for all Linux discussions. To find out more about Linux from the internet, browse `http://www.linux.org`. Figure 1.3 is an example of this Web page as it appeared during the writing of this book.

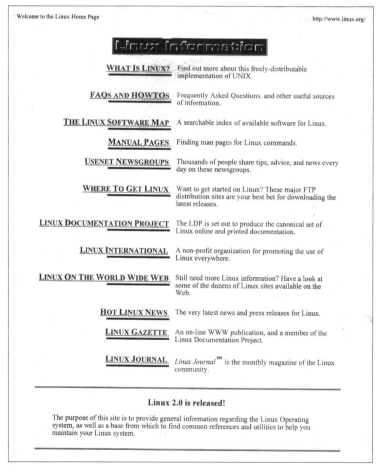

**Figure 1.3.** *Linux organization home Web page*

Linux has a tremendous following, with the number of sites estimated at more than half a million. Linux is continuously being updated by people all over the world. The entire GNU utility library and X-windows has been ported to Linux. Linux has a DOS emulator allowing it to run DOS programs. Since its inception, the number of available applications for Linux has increased tremendously. Linux is under the GNU *General Public License* (GPL). The GPL guarantees the Linux sources are always available for you to modify, copy, and distribute. Linux is discussed in this book because of its immense popularity.

## Solaris

Solaris is Sun Microsystems' flagship System V-based 32-bit operating system designed to run on several different platforms. As this book was being written, Version 2.5.1 was the latest version of Solaris. It supported the following platforms: SPARC, UltraSPARC, Intel 486, Pentium, Pentium Pro, and PowerPC. This version of Solaris is the first to be deployed on both the SPARC and UltraSPARC architectures. SunSoft, the division of Sun Microsystems that produces Solaris, is now committed to a 64-bit architecture. Future versions of Solaris will continue to evolve toward 64-bit architectures, but will continue to support 32-bit applications. Solaris programs can use up to 3.75 GB of virtual memory. Solaris is a very scalable operating system, able to run on anything from 1 to 64 processors. The Solaris user environment is based on the Open Look (OpenWindows) graphical user interface. Solaris also supports the *Common Desktop Environment* (CDE), which provides a transparent interoperable windows-oriented GUI environment. The Solaris Desktop also includes the *Windows Access Binary Interface* (WABI), which allows users to run Microsoft Windows applications such as Microsoft Office and the Lotus SmartSuite. WABI supports multimedia and *Open Database Connect* (ODBC) applications. Sun maintains a comprehensive Web site containing all of the latest information about Solaris at `http://www.sun.com`. With the proliferation of Sun workstations over the past several years, Solaris is becoming one of the most widely used versions of UNIX.

# Chapter 2

# The User Interface

UNIX and Windows both provide command-line and graphical user interfaces. This chapter focuses on the GUI differences among Windows NT, Windows 95, Solaris, and Linux. Version 7.0 MS-DOS windows can be created in the Microsoft Windows environments, enabling users to enter command-line style commands. Linux also contains a DOS emulator, allowing it to run MS-DOS commands. Although the majority of system operations can be performed by pointing and clicking with a mouse, some users may wish to perform certain system functions directly at a command-line prompt. Also, many legacy applications require the use of the traditional MS-DOS command-line environment. Some of the command-line interfaces are contrasted in Appendix B. The following questions about the GUI environment for Windows 95/NT and UNIX OpenWindows for Solaris and Linux are answered in this chapter:

## The Desktop

- How do you use the mouse to manipulate objects on the desktop?
- How is information organized on the desktop?
- How do you change the characteristics of the desktop?
- How do you launch programs from the desktop?

## File Management

- How are file types iconified by large or small icons?
- How do you sort files by name, size, or date?

- How do you create new shortcuts, documents, and folders?
- How do you copy, move, and rename files?
- How do you search for files?
- How do you delete files, and recover them from a wastebasket facility?
- How do you obtain information about a file (such as permissions)?
- How do you change file attributes?
- How do you create a hierarchical folder view?

## The Calendar

- How do you activate the calendar tool?
- How do you register appointments with the calendar tool?
- How do you navigate time periods?

## The Calculator

- How do you change between scientific and standard mode?
- How do you change between different numeric bases?

## The Clock

- How do you change the style of the clock from digital to analog to Roman?
- How do you change the clock from 12-hour to 24-hour?
- How do you change the time zone?
- How do you set alarms?

## On-Line Help

- How do you get help from the desktop?

## Mail

- How is the mail utility activated?
- How is mail sent and received with the mail utility?

## User Accessibility

- What kinds of user accessibility exist for people challenged by using the keyboard and mouse to interact with the system?

## Microsoft Windows — The Desktop

As of Version 4.0 of Windows NT, the look and feel of the GUI is identical to that found in Windows 95. Figure 2.1 illustrates the typical layout of a Windows 95 desktop. The pop-up screen for a V4.0 Windows NT Workstation looks virtually identical to a Windows 95 pop-up screen and is depicted in Figure 2.2.

**Figure 2.1.** *A Windows 95 desktop*

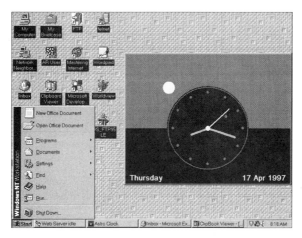

**Figure 2.2.** *Pop-up menu from clicking on START button in Windows NT Workstation Version 4.0*

The **Programs** choice displays more menus listing other programs available to run. Figure 2.3 illustrates what happens when you move the mouse pointer over the **Programs** area of the pop-up menu. It is not necessary to click to activate the program menus.

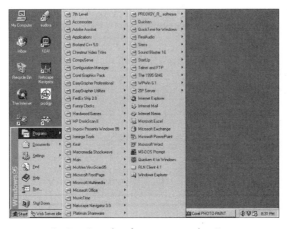

**Figure 2.3.** *Result of activating the Program menu*

Because the GUIs of Windows 95 and Windows NT V4.0 are similar, most illustrations are from a Windows 95 system. Windows NT appears in illustrations only where it is unique. The GUI desktop area contains a collection of icons representing shortcuts. You can double-click the shortcut icons to activate the particular program they represent. At the bottom of the screen is the task bar. The task bar contains the START button, and various other indicators depending on current system activity. The START button is used to activate other menus that list programs to run. Clicking on the START button on a Windows 95 system causes the pop-up menu depicted in Figure 2.4 to appear.

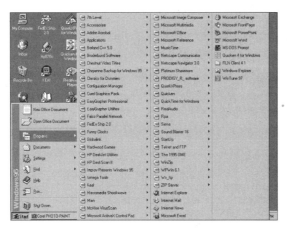

**Figure 2.4.** *Pop-up menu from clicking on START button in Windows 95*

Many of the items in the **Programs** menu also can be expanded into still more levels of menus. Consider Figure 2.5, where **Corel Graphics Pack** is selected, and another menu list is produced. The user then clicks on one of these items in this final menu level to activate one of the Corel programs.

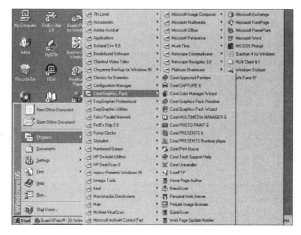

**Figure 2.5.** *Selecting the* ***Corel Graphics Pack*** *menu*

The **Documents** menu choice produces a list of the latest series of documents that have been edited with any word processor or image manipulation utility. Figure 2.6 illustrates the result of selecting the **Documents** menu. A small icon appears next to the file name indicating the characteristic of the file.

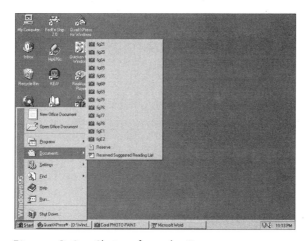

**Figure 2.6.** *Choices from the* ***Documents*** *menu*

The **Settings** menu allows you to activate the **Control Panel** screen. The **Control Panel** is used to manage the system and consists of the facilities illustrated in Figure 2.7. From within the **Control Panel**, you can control the appearance of the desktop, change hardware attributes, and remove and install software. Other choices from the **Settings** menu allow you to go directly to the **Printers** menu or the taskbar menu. The **Printers** menu is used to add, remove, or change printers. The taskbar menu allows you to customize the use of the taskbar. Figure 2.8 illustrates the taskbar menu and what characteristics can be changed.

**Figure 2.7.** *Contents of the **Control Panel** menu*

**Figure 2.8.** *The taskbar menu*

The remaining items on the pop-up menu are **Help**, **Run**, and **Shutdown**. Clicking on **Help** provides you with a comprehensive collection of on-line documentation about every aspect of the system. The **Run** selection allows you to select a specific program to run, either by browsing for it or by manually entering the name of the program file. The **Shutdown** selection allows you to shut the system down to power off, or to restart the system either in Windows 95/NT or to an MS-DOS prompt.

Windows takes advantage of having more than one mouse button and causes different action depending on what button is clicked. The button orientation here is discussed with respect to a right-handed individual. The left mouse button is normally used to select items from the desktop. However, the right mouse button can be used to activate different menus. Right-clicking anywhere on the desktop that is not over a shortcut produces the menu illustrated in Figure 2.9.

**Figure 2.9.** *Result of right-clicking mouse over the desktop*

This is a quick way of aligning the shortcut icons and for getting into the display characteristics menu by clicking on **Properties**. Right-clicking on a shortcut produces a different result, as seen in Figure 2.10. The Netscape shortcut has been selected and can be manipulated according to the action items listed.

Right-clicking on the **Start** button also produces a different effect than left-clicking, as seen in Figure 2.11. By clicking on **Open**, you get a window full of icons representing programs situated on the **Programs** menu. By moving program icons into and out of this window, you can control what programs appear in the **Programs** menu list. **Explore** and **Find** are two other utilities for managing files. **Explore** is the evolution of the former File Manager from the

Windows 3.X world, and **Find** is a manifestation of the former File
Manager search option. If a virus scanner is installed on the system,
that may be activated from here as well.

**Figure 2.10.** *Result of right-clicking the mouse over a desktop shortcut.
Shortcut in this figure is Netscape Navigator.*

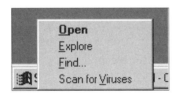

**Figure 2.11.** *Result of right-clicking over the Start button*

The **System Agents** area of the desktop will vary depending on
what options are installed on the system. Figure 2.12 illustrates the
**System Agents** icon area.

**Figure 2.12.** *System agents icons. From left to right,* speaker volume, McAfee
Virus Scanner, Microsoft Plus! Agents, *and* the time of day (10:53 PM)

Window sizing is accomplished by moving the mouse pointer over any
side or corner of a window. The mouse changes into a two-headed
arrow pointing according to the side/corner orientation. When the
arrow is the desired shape, clicking and holding the left mouse button

will alter that dimension of the window until the left mouse button is released. Windows can also be iconified to the taskbar, maximized to fill the entire screen, or deleted from the desktop by clicking one of the three buttons present in the upper right-hand corner of every window structure. Figure 2.13 illustrates these three buttons.

**Figure 2.13.** *Window iconification/maximizing/deleting buttons found in upper right-hand corner of all window frames*

Other characteristics of the desktop can be customized from the pop-up menu depicted in Figure 2.10. Clicking on the **Properties** item produces the window in Figure 2.14.

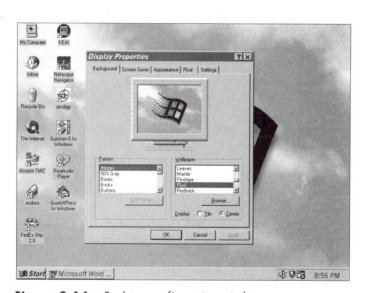

**Figure 2.14.** *Desktop configuration window*

From this window a user can select the following:

- Background
- Screen Saver
- Appearance
- Microsoft Plus!
- Settings

Clicking the **Background** tab allows the desktop background to be according to a pattern, such as bricks or buttons, or a wallpaper, such as leaves or marble. Clicking the **Screen Saver** tab allows choosing a screen saver. The screen saver choices will vary depending on what screen savers are installed on the system in addition to the ones that come with Windows. Clicking the **Appearance** tab allows you to control the color and depiction of windows, window borders, and menu bars. Clicking the **Plus!** tab allows choosing a desktop theme if the Microsoft Plus! option is installed. Clicking the **Settings** tab allows control of various video characteristics such as number of colors, font size, and display type.

The **Regional Settings** icon in the **Control Panel** window controls what country and language should be used on the system. The **Regional Settings** window is also discussed with respect to the clock. The **Regional Settings** window is depicted in Figure 2.15.

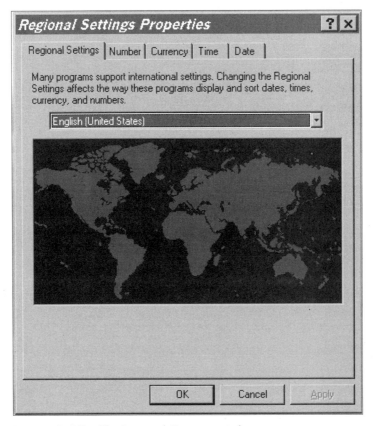

**Figure 2.15.** *The Regional Settings window*

## Microsoft Windows — File Management

File management has been made exceedingly easy with the point-and-click philosophy of Windows. The GUI eliminates the need to tediously enter file commands and file names. This is especially convenient when you consider that Windows 95 and Windows NT V4.0 allow long file names! The major file management tool in Microsoft Windows for both Windows 95 and Windows NT Version 4.0 is Explorer. Explorer can be activated in two ways: by right-clicking over the **Start** button, or from the **Programs** menu.

Explorer has many options that control how the file information is displayed. Figure 2.16 is an example of a short icon listing. Figure 2.17 is an example of a large icon listing. Explorer attempts to characterize the files with icons that visually facilitate file identification. Right-clicking over the icons or the file names depicted in the left-hand portion of the display produces a menu like that in Figure 2.10.

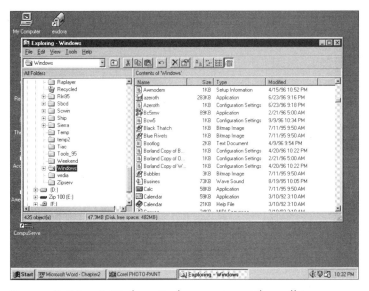

**Figure 2.16.** *A Windows Explorer screen with small icons*

A file listed by either the small-icon or the large-icon method can easily be moved to the desktop by moving the mouse button over the file of interest, clicking once, holding down the left mouse button, and dragging to anywhere on the desktop. The icon now becomes a shortcut.

**Figure 2.17.** *A Windows Explorer screen with large icons*

The Explorer screen is divided into several sections, as depicted in
Figures 2.16 and 2.17. Along the top of the screen is a window indicating the current directory. In the figures, Windows is the current
directory, as shown by the fact that the directory Windows is highlighted in the **All Folders** window. By double-clicking a directory
folder in the **All Folders** window, you get a display of the contents of
that folder on the right-hand side in the **Contents of...** window. At
the bottom of the screen are indicators for how many file objects were
found in this directory, how much disk space is occupied by these files,
and how much overall disk space is still available on the current drive.

Windows Explorer can also be used to map a networked disk
drive by using the pull-down menu **Tools** and selecting **Map
Network Drive**. The user is prompted for a server, a service, and,
optionally, a drive letter. Networked drives appear as local disk drives,
and file views from them are indistinguishable from those obtained
from the local hard drive.

## Microsoft Windows — Calendar Management

The calendar tool under Microsoft Windows 95 and Windows NT
appears as Figure 2.18. The current day is darkened. By clicking on
the arrows between the time and date bar, a user can show previous

or subsequent months. Double-clicking on any of the days produces a
window depicting a schedule, as illustrated in Figure 2.19.

   Entries in the schedule can be alarmed to produce an audible
reminder of an appointment. More elaborate scheduling capability is
available with Microsoft Exchange. The version of Exchange that comes
with Windows 95 and Windows NT does not contain any scheduling
capability. A more elaborate version of Exchange is available that performs a wide variety of scheduling functions, all integrated with mail.

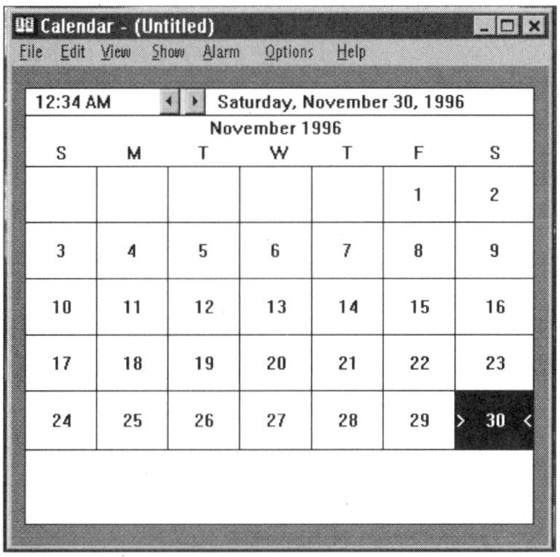

**Figure 2.18.** *Microsoft Windows calendar tool*

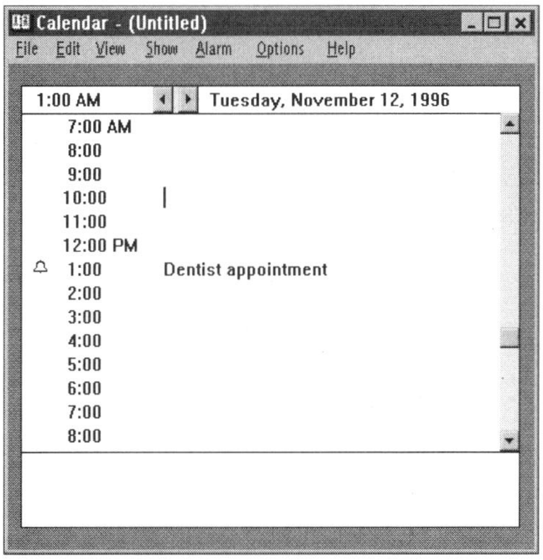

**Figure 2.19.** *Result of clicking on a day in the Calendar Manager display with
an alarmed entry*

## Microsoft Windows — The Calculator Tool

The calculator tool in Microsoft Windows 95 and Windows NT is invoked from the Accessories menu and appears as in Figure 2.20.

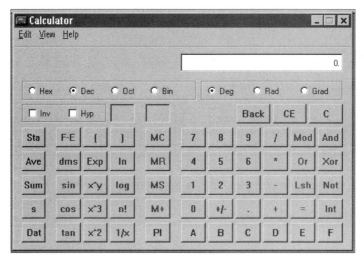

**Figure 2.20.** *Microsoft Windows Calculator Tool, scientific version*

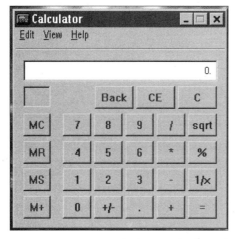

**Figure 2.21.** *Standard version of Microsoft Windows Calculator Tool*

The Calculator Tool can also be activated in standard form, as shown in Figure 2.21. The change between scientific and standard forms is accomplished by making the desired selection from the **View** pull-down menu.

## Microsoft Windows — Exchange

The mail facility available in both Windows 95 and Windows NT is Exchange. A more elaborate version of Exchange can be purchased that contains a very robust integrated scheduling component. The Exchange utility is a standard fixture of the desktop and appears as the Inbox icon. Figure 2.22 illustrates the window resulting from double-clicking on the Inbox icon.

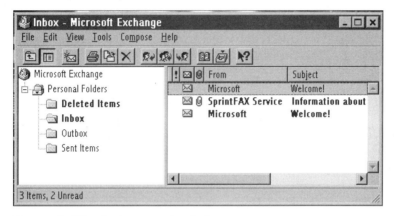

**Figure 2.22.** *Exchange main window*

The Exchange main window is divided into two sections. The list of folders appears on the left-hand side, and the contents of the selected open folder appear on the right-hand side. In Figure 2.22, folder Inbox is open and the contents of **Inbox** are displayed in the right window. Specific mail messages are opened by double-clicking on the envelope icons in the right window. Envelope icons that appear with a paper clip imply an attachment with the message. Figure 2.23 illustrates the toolbar buttons and their meaning. When Exchange is running and there is mail waiting to be read, a small icon depicting a letter appears in the System Agents area, as illustrated in Figure 2.24.

**Figure 2.23.** *The Exchange mail utility tool bar: (a) up one folder level, (b) show/hide folders, (c) send a message, (d) print message, (e) move message, (f) delete message, (g) reply, (h) reply to all, (i) forward, (j) address book, (k) inbox, and (l) help*

**Figure 2.24.** *System agents area indicating mail waiting from Exchange*

## Microsoft Windows — The Clock Utility

The clock utility is initiated from the **Accessories** submenu. Figure 2.25 depicts the display from the clock utility. Figure 2.25a is how the clock utility display looks by default. Figure 2.25b shows the results of clicking on the **Settings** item. The clock can be set to display time in analog or digital style, without a title, with a seconds indicator, and with or without the date.

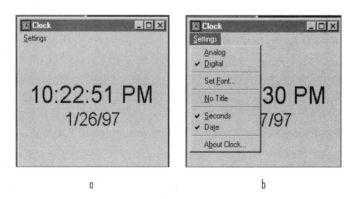

a                                    b

**Figure 2.25.** *The windows clock utility: (a) clock default analog display; (b) clock settings menu*

Double-clicking anywhere on the clock face removes the top bar title. There is no means for setting an alarm with the clock utility. Date and time alarms are available with optional software such as the scheduler that comes with Microsoft Exchange.

The system time in windows can be set by right-clicking with the mouse on the time field in the **System Agents** area of the desktop. Clicking on the **Adjust Date/Time** item produces the window depicted in Figure 2.26. This menu allows the user to set the time and date, as well as to specify the time zone. Time and date formats can be customized by going into the **Regional Settings** from the **Control Panel**. Within the **Regional Settings** menu, time format can be established for 24-hour or 12-hour time.

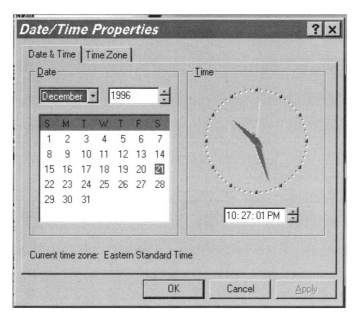

**Figure 2.26.** *Adjusting the time and date in Microsoft windows*

## Microsoft Windows — On-Line Help

Microsoft Windows has an abundance of on-line help. Help is always available from the Start button. Clicking on the **Help** item in the pop-up menu displays the menu in Figure 2.27.

The system automatically matches your help request with the display list. The matching is approximate; a best match for the request is attempted, and the topic's description line is highlighted. You can obtain detailed information by clicking on the **Display** button at the bottom of the help window. You can also manually scroll through the list by using the mouse on the scroll bar on the right-hand side of the display window.

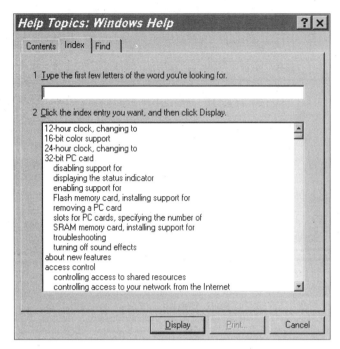

**Figure 2.27.** *The main help screen in Microsoft Windows*

## The Command-Line Interface in Microsoft Windows

Users can open a Version 7.0 MS-DOS window and key in commands
to the system through it. A table summarizing the most frequently
used of these commands, along with the corresponding commands in
UNIX and the GUI environments of both operating systems, is presented in Appendix B at the end of this book.

## UNIX — Solaris

Solaris users employ OpenWindows, which is based on the Open
Look GUI. Figure 2.28 illustrates a Solaris workspace.

Solaris takes advantage of all the buttons on a mouse, whether it
has three buttons or two. Figure 2.29 illustrates which mouse buttons
perform which actions. The mouse button functions are key to using
the OpenWindows workspace effectively. The workspace menu is
obtained by clicking the **MENU** button anywhere on the workspace.
Figure 2.30a illustrates the workspace submenu.

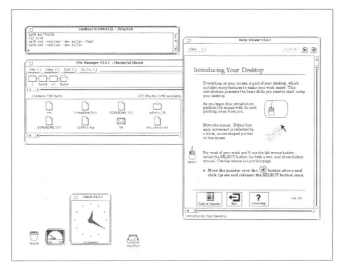

**Figure 2.28.** *Basic Solaris OpenWindows workspace*

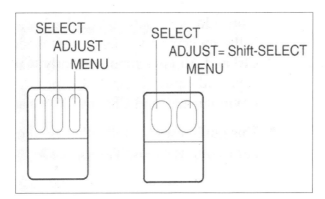

**Figure 2.29.** *Solaris mouse button functions* (Copyright 1994 Sun Microsystems Inc. Used by permission.)

The Solaris OpenWindows environment has a feature with no equivalent in the Microsoft Windows world: pinning a menu. A *push-pin* is actually apparent in the upper left corner of some windows. A window can actually be pinned onto the desktop by clicking and holding the **MENU** button and moving the mouse pointer over the push-pin. Once the pin is pushed in, the menu always stays up. You can see the push-pin in Figure 2.30.

Programs are activated by displaying the **Workspace** menu, Figure 2.30a, and moving the mouse pointer over **Programs** and clicking the **MENU** button. Figure 2.30b illustrates the results of selecting the **Programs** menu.

a                                                b

**Figure 2.30.** *(a) The Workspace menu, and (b) the Programs menu*

The OpenWindows drag and drop feature allows you to move files conveniently between applications. Usually files are dragged from a file manager window and dropped onto another application such as the editor. To choose the file, move the pointer over the file icon and click **SELECT**. If additional files are to be moved, moving the pointer over them and clicking **ADJUST** will select them as well. By pressing the **SELECT** key, you can move the files to their target, which is usually designated as a rectangle in the upper right-hand corner of the application window. The rectangle will appear clear when no file has been loaded and turn dark when a file has been loaded. Figure 2.31 illustrates this effect with the Print tool.

Although the drag and drop feature is not available with all applications, various combinations of applications can use this feature.

For example, file manager glyphs can be dropped onto the following:

- The Mail Tool
- The Print Tool
- The Text Editor
- The Audio Tool

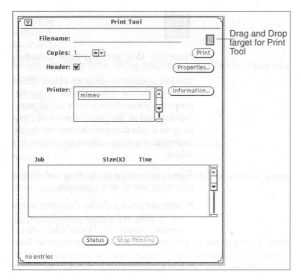

**Figure 2.31.** *OpenWindows drag and drop target box* (Copyright 1994 Sun Microsystems Inc. Used by permission.)

Mail messages from the Mail tool can be dropped onto the following:

- The File Manager
- The Wastebasket
- The Calendar Manager

You can resize OpenWindows windows by positioning the pointer on one of the windows corners, pressing **SELECT**, and moving the pointer to change the size of the window. Once the desired size is attained, release the **SELECT** button. Figure 2.32 illustrates the resizing corners.

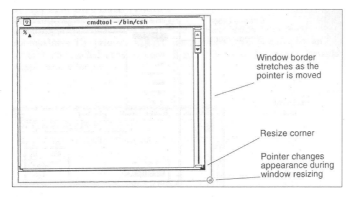

**Figure 2.32.** *Changing the window size in OpenWindows* (Copyright 1994 Sun Microsystems Inc. Used by permission.)

Other characteristics of the workstation environment can be customized by clicking on the **Properties** submenu from the **Workspace** menu. The properties choices will vary according to the workstation hardware configuration. **Workspace** properties are changed initially from the **Categories** menu, which is depicted in Figure 2.33.

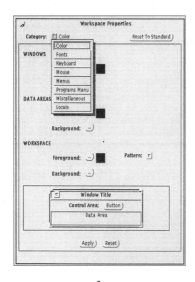     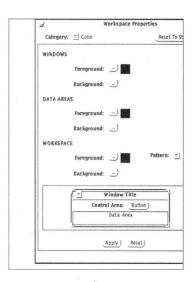

a                                        b

**Figure 2.33.** *The Workspace properties Category menu (a) before categories are selected and (b) when categories are selected*

The **Category** menu allows a user to adjust the following workspace properties:

*Color*
Windows, data areas, and workspace foreground and background; window title can also be set from here

*Fonts*
Font scale and style

*Keyboard*
Set keyboard accelerator keys

*Mouse*
Acceleration, threshold, multiclick interval, and pointer jumping

**Menus**
    Drag-right distance and left-mouse press

**Programs menu**
    Allows you to add items to your Programs menu

**Miscellaneous**
    Turn screen saver on or off, when to beep, icon locations, scroll bar
    placement

**Locale**
    Country and language

## Solaris Calendar Manager

The Calendar Manager (CM) is a convenient utility for keeping track
of appointments. The CM is integrated with mail, allowing you to
notify other users about appointments. The CM is activated from the
**Programs** menu and initially appears in icon form as depicted in
Figure 2.34. The current day is presented by default.

**Figure 2.34.** *The Calendar Manager in its initial display form*

When you double-click on the CM icon with the **SELECT** button, the current month is presented by default, as illustrated by
Figure 2.35. Any appointments will also be listed for the appropriate days. Various menu commands are available along the top of the
CM window. The **View** menu allows you to choose the month,
week, and day views. This menu also allows you to select a time
zone, find an appointment, or go to a selected date, as shown in
Figure 2.36. The **Edit** menu allows you to schedule appointments
and manage the **To Do** list. The CM can also be used strictly as a
reminder tool not associated with remembering appointments. The
**Browse** menu allows you to view calendars from other users. The

**Print** menu allows you to print the currently selected view. To view future or previous days, click on the navigation controls (**Prev**, **Today**, and **Next**) situated in the upper right-hand corner of the calendar window.

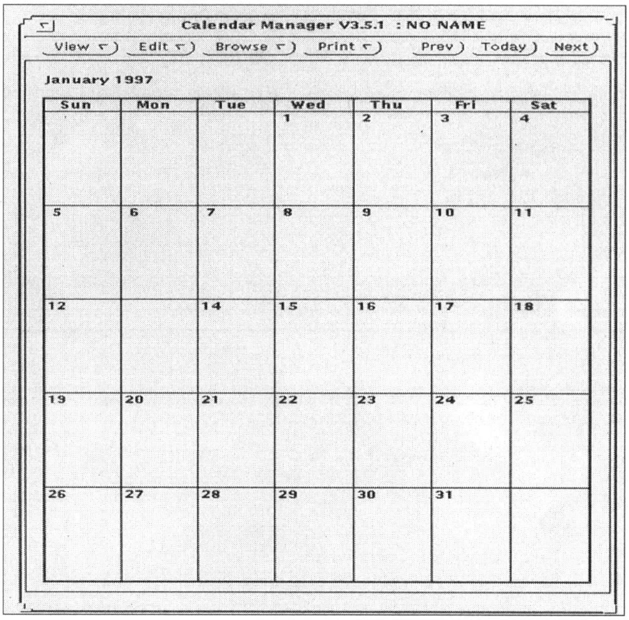

**Figure 2.35.** *Result of invoking the Calendar manager icon*

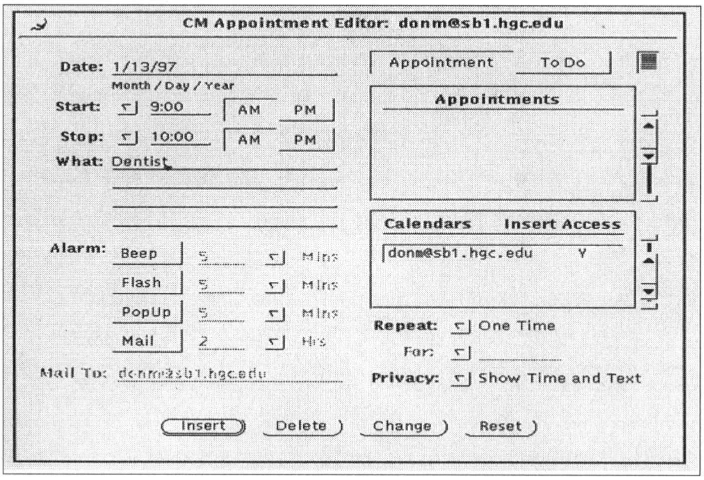

**Figure 2.36.** *CM alarm and appointment setup window*

## Solaris DeskSet Calculator

The Solaris DeskSet Calculator is a versatile tool that lets you perform computation for business and finance and in various numeric modes. The calculator is activated by selecting Calculator from the **Program** submenu. Figure 2.37 illustrates the layout of the calculator tool.

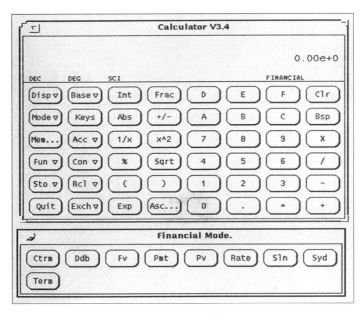

**Figure 2.37.** *The Solaris DeskSet calculator with Financial Mode button set*

The numeric bases can be selected by clicking **SELECT** on the **Base** ∇ button on the left-hand side of the calculator face. The modes available are binary, octal, decimal, and hexidecimal. The calculator can also be adjusted to display data in three different modes:

- Engineering
- Fixed point
- Scientific

Select the display style by clicking the **Disp** ∇ button with the **SELECT** button and moving the pointer to the display style of choice. Choose calculator modes by clicking the **SELECT** button on the **Mode** ∇ button. The four modes are as follows:

- Basic
- Financial
- Logical
- Scientific

The **Basic** mode is what is established by default at activation time. The other three mode selections cause a pop-up window to appear with additional keys. Other keys on the calculator are typically found on real calculators, such as **Sto∇**, **Rcl∇**, **Mem∇** and **Exch∇**. The **Exch∇** key swaps the contents of the current display with the current memory register value. User defined functions can also be established by clicking on the **Fun∇** key. The additional keys for the other three calculator modes are illustrated in Figure 2.38.

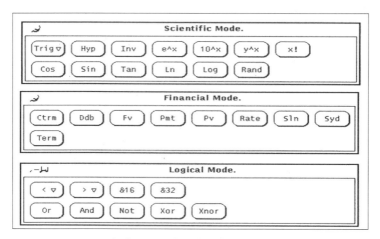

**Figure 2.38.** *Calculator modes: from top, scientific mode, financial mode, and logical mode*

## The Solaris Clock Application

The Solaris Clock Application is activated from the **Programs** submenu off the **Workspace** menu. The clock face depicted in Figure 2.39 is typically displayed in icon form.

The clock in icon form can be displayed with no numerals or with Roman numerals. The Solaris clock can be significantly customized. Clicking on the **MENU** button while the pointer is anywhere over the clock face produces a **Properties** menu choice.

Clicking on the **Properties** choice creates the properties window shown in Figure 2.40.

**Figure 2.39.** *The icon-form clock face from Solaris clock application*

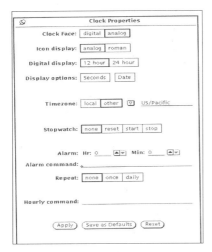

**Figure 2.40.** *The Solaris clock properties window*

Within the clock properties window, a user can control a wide variety of clock characteristics, including the following:

- Digital or analog display
- Display with Roman numerals
- Icon display in analog form
- 12-hour or 24-hour display
- Display seconds
- Display date
- Display time zone
- Initiate stopwatch options
- Set an alarm

## Solaris Mail Tool

The mail tool is activated from the **Programs** menu. Mail tool icons vary in appearance depending on whether mail is present or not. Figure 2.41 illustrates the three possible icon configurations.

a           b          c

**Figure 2.41.** *Mail Tool icon configurations: (a) no mail, (b) no new mail, (c) new mail*

Clicking on the icon in Figure 2.41b creates the window shown in Figure 2.42.

**Figure 2.42.** *Result of clicking on the Mail Tool icon: the scrolling list of mail messages*

The mail list is organized into several fields: the *message number*, *message source address*, *delivery day and time*, *number of lines/number of characters,* and *subject message header.*

## OpenWindows File Manager in Solaris

The Solaris OpenWindows file manager can display file information in a variety of ways. Two examples demonstrated here are with large icons, as illustrated in Figure 2.43, and with small icons as illustrated in Figure 2.44.

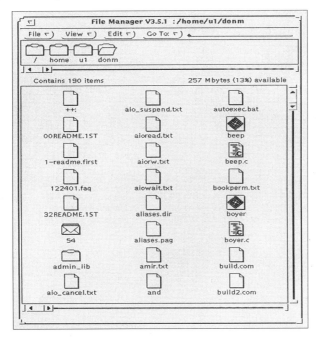

**Figure 2.43.** *Solaris OpenWindows file manager with large icons*

As you can see in Figure 2.43, the file manager attempts to graphically represent the nature of the files. Directories and text files appear as file folders. Executable programs appear as the Sun logo box. C programs appear as file folders with a .C displayed on the cover. The user's mailbox appears as a group of envelope icons. The number beneath the envelope GUI represents how many messages are in the mail box.

Figure 2.44 illustrates a Solaris file manager screen displaying small icons.

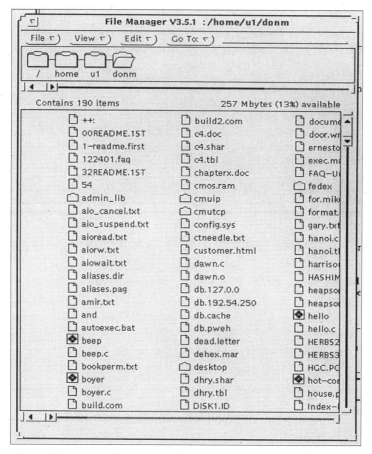

**Figure 2.44.** *Solaris file manager showing small file icons*

## Solaris On-Line Help

There are several sources of help in the Solaris environment.

- UNIX man pages
- General help from the **Workspace** menu
- AnswerBook Navigator

UNIX man pages work like conventional UNIX man pages. If the exact spelling of the man page command subject is questionable, the man -k [keyword] (-k means keyword search) command can be used to seek out all related topics.

The general help facility from the **Workspace** menu provides information on a variety of topics about the desktop, including AnswerBook. The general help facility is a good way to familiarize yourself with the desktop: by reading the first page, titled *Desktop Intro to Handbook*.

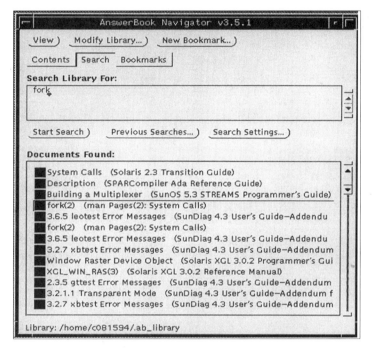

**Figure 2.45.** *The AnswerBook Navigator initial page*

AnswerBook, if installed by your system administrator, is activated from the **Programs** submenu from the **Workspace** menu. The AnswerBook Navigator appears initially to let you specify topic search criteria. The AnswerBook Navigator can be seen in Figure 2.45. Once a topic is chosen, the AnswerBook Viewer appears displaying the topic information and can be seen in Figure 2.46. The display is *wysiwyg* and appears exactly as it would in a printed manual. AnswerBook allows you to establish bookmarks to facilitate returning to a particular discussion. AnswerBook can also be customized to reference information particular to your login environment. This customization is primarily used to streamline AnswerBook performance. AnswerBook is by far the best help facility you will find in Solaris, because it provides context-sensitive information.

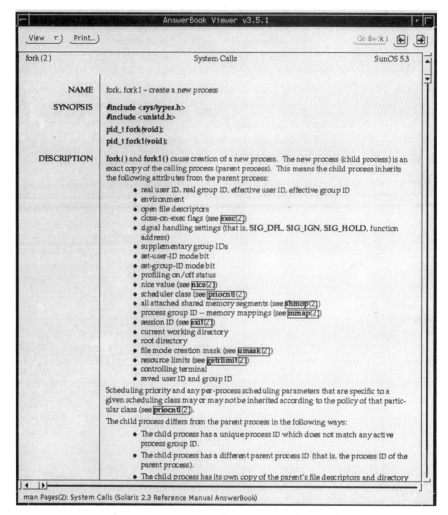

**Figure 2.46.** *Information about the fork function derived from the AnswerBook Navigator*

## OpenWindows Linux File Manager

The OpenWindows GUI tools in Linux resemble those found in Solaris. The Linux GUI environment is produced with XView. Figure 2.47 illustrates a typical large-icon file manager display.

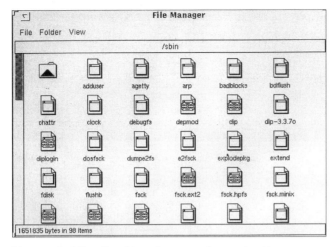

**Figure 2.47.** *The file manager utility under Linux*

Figure 2.48 is another depiction of the file manager under Linux. In Figure 2.48 we have selected a file (note the box around file glyph), have right-clicked the mouse, and have selected Permissions, producing the box in the upper right-hand corner.

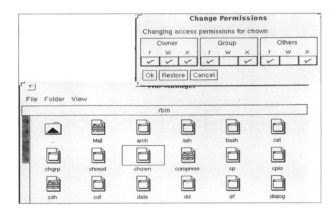

**Figure 2.48.** *Linux file manager with file glyph selected for Permissions adjustment*

## Solaris and Linux — Searching for Files

The OpenWindows environment provides several ways to search for files with the file manager:

- The **Go to** menu
- The **Find** pop-up window
- Pattern matching in file manager window

Clicking on the **Go to** menu and selecting **Text** lets you enter the name of a file or folder. The name can include the entire path name pointing to the file or folder. The **Go to** menu also includes the list of files and folders that have been accessed since you started the file manager.

The **Find** pop-up window is activated from the file manager **File** menu by selecting **Find**. The Find facility lets you refine the search by specifying file types, the file owner, and file modification times. Find even allows you to search for files containing a specific string. The **Find** window appears in Figure 2.49.

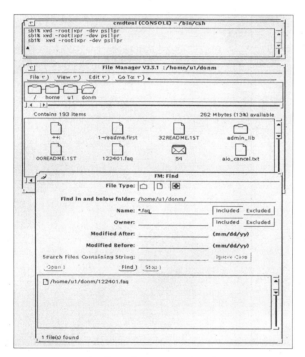

**Figure 2.49.** *The File Manager Find window*

The final method used to search for files is by pattern matching in the File Manager window. You can start typing the name of the file or folder for which you are searching by moving the pointer anywhere over the File Manager window. As you enter the file name, the system will display all of the files or folders that match what you have entered so far. This pattern-matching technique can also be performed within the **Go to** menu.

## Searching for Files — Microsoft Windows

File searching in Windows 95 and Windows NT can be performed in two ways:

- By right-clicking on the **Start** button and selecting **Find**
- By activating the Explore utility and selecting **Find** from the **Tools** menu

The **Find** utility window appears in Figure 2.50.

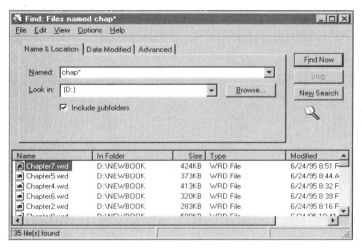

**Figure 2.50.** *The Microsoft Windows Find window*

Figure 2.50 shows the **Find** utility after it has found all occurrences of files whose names start with the characters "chap." The **Find** window can be resized to display more information about the files, such as modification times, size, and current folder location. You can sort the files-found window by clicking on the buttons with the column titles. For example, continuously clicking on the **Size** button will sort the data, alternating between listing files from largest to smallest and listing them from smallest to largest. You can exclude subfolders from the search by not clicking the **Include subfolders** box.

## Solaris — Access for Users with Disabilities

The AccessX extension is used in the Solaris environment to accommodate users with disabilities. AccessX facilitates using the mouse and keyboard by providing a variety of visual and audio cues. AccessX provides for the following features:

- StickyKeys
- MouseKeys
- ToggleKeys
- RepeatKeys
- SlowKeys
- BounceKeys

The **AccessX - Settings...** window appears as shown in Figure 2.51.

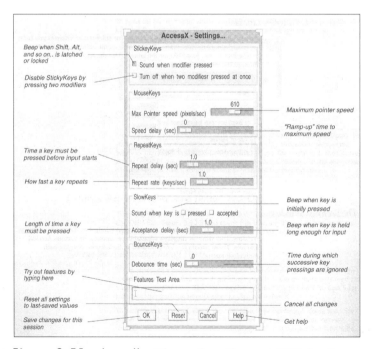

**Figure 2.51.** *AccessX setting options* (Copyright 1994 Sun Microsystems Inc. Used by permission.)

**StickyKeys** are used to accommodate users who have difficulty holding down two keys at once, such as Control-D or Shift-Mouse-click. StickyKeys allow such keys as the Shift, Alt, or Control keys, called *modifier keys*, to stay active while another key is typed. StickyKeys can be established so that when a modifier key is pressed, a beep is produced.

**MouseKeys** are used when using a mouse is difficult. MouseKeys involve using the numeric keypad to perform the motions of a mouse. Figure 2.52 illustrates the kinds of control created with MouseKeys on the numeric keypad.

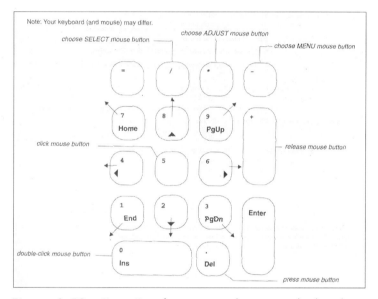

**Figure 2.52.** *MouseKeys functions on the numeric keyboard* (COPYRIGHT 1994 SUN MICROSYSTEMS INC. USED BY PERMISSION.)

**ToggleKeys** are an aural cue mechanism to replace LEDS found on keyboards that indicate that certain functions are in effect. For example, pressing the Num Lock key would produce a single beep; deactivating the key would produce two beeps.

**RepeatKeys** are for users with limited motor skills who have a hard time removing their fingers from a key and cause unwanted repetition of the keystroke. When RepeatKeys are in effect, a key must be held down for a specific period of time before it will repeat.

**SlowKeys** are handy for users who frequently hit the wrong key, for example, hitting the *w* instead of the *e*. When SlowKeys are in effect, a key must be held down for a specific period of time before it is recognized.

**BounceKeys** are used to control users who have difficulty holding down a key or who repeatedly strike a key when they mean to hit it once. BounceKeys make the system ignore rapid repeated keystrokes.

## Microsoft Windows Accessibility Options

The Microsoft Windows user accessibility options are accessed through the Control Panel. By clicking on the **Accessibility Options** icon illustrated in Figure 2.53, the window in Figure 2.54 is produced.

**Figure 2.53.** *Accessibility icon as it appears in the control panel*

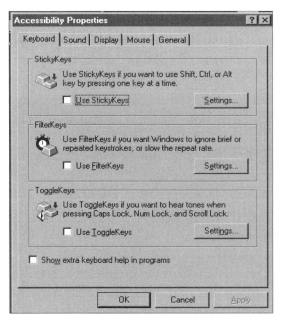

**Figure 2.54.** *The Accessibility Options Properties screen*

Microsoft Windows provides controls for the *keyboard*, *sound*, *display*, *mouse*, and a *general category*. The **Keyboard** tab lets you control activating **StickyKeys**, **FilterKeys**, and **ToggleKeys**. These options are similar to what is available in the Solaris environment. **StickyKeys** are used to help you enter keyboard sequences requiring the pressing of two keys, such as Control-C. **FilterKeys** allow controlling how Windows recognizes brief or repeated keystrokes. ToggleKeys are used to produce an audible signal when certain keys are pressed, such as the Num Lock or Caps keys. Figure 2.55 illustrates the StickyKeys options.

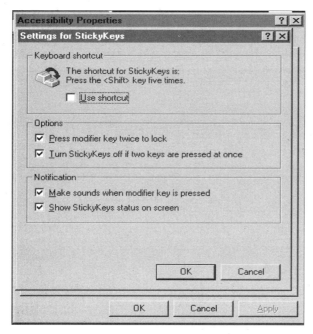

**Figure 2.55.** *The StickyKeys setting window*

The **Sounds** tab produces the window seen in Figure 2.56 and lets you specify various aural cues. The Sounds tab window can be used to cause the system or your programs to produce visual captions when a sound is produced.

The **Display** tab controls the degree of contrast of the console display. The **Mouse** tab allows the activation of **MouseKeys**. Figure 2.57 illustrates the contents of the **MouseKeys** window.

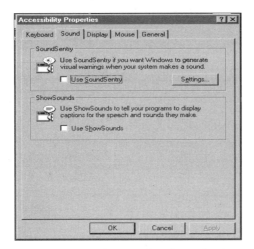

**Figure 2.56.** *The Sounds tab window*

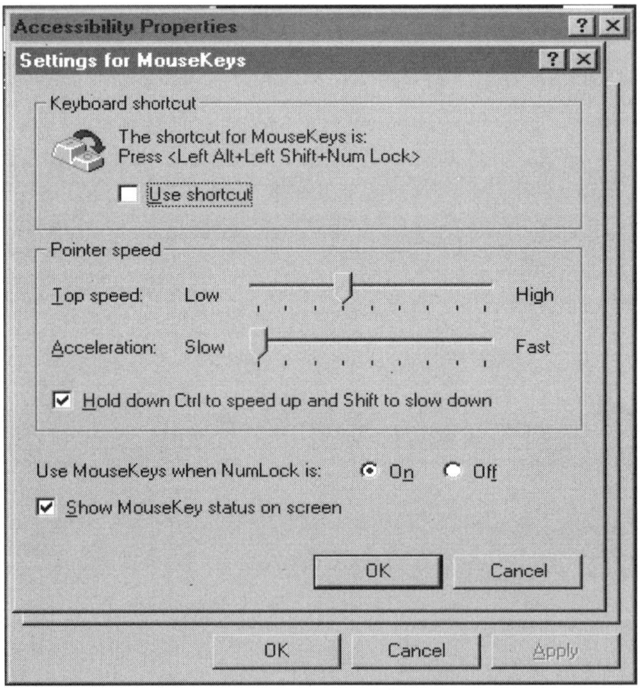

**Figure 2.57.** *The MouseKeys control window*

The **General** tab produces the window illustrated in Figure
2.58. This window lets you activate aural cues that sound when features are turned on or off, and also lets you specify how SerialKey
devices can be used as an alternative means of accessing mouse and
keyboard features. A COM port and baud are specified in this window.

The **General** tab also allows the system to be set to automatically disable the accessibility features for a specified idle time.

**Figure 2.58.** *The contents of the Accessibility Properties General tab*

## UNIX — Solaris: Controlling Mouse Properties

Solaris mouse behavior is controlled through the **Workspace Properties** window by selecting **Mouse** as the Category. The display in Figure 2.59 is presented. Several mouse characteristics can be controlled, including the following:

| | |
|---|---|
| *Acceleration* | Controls the speed of the mouse |
| *Click interval* | Time in tenths of a second to distinguish a double-click from a single click |
| *Button order* | Changes meaning of mouse buttons for what is **SELECT**, **MENU**, and **ADJUST** |
| *Pointer jumping* | Determines how the mouse pointer moves relative to a scrolling window or pop-up menu |
| *Threshold* | Determines how many pixels the mouse must move to determine acceleration |

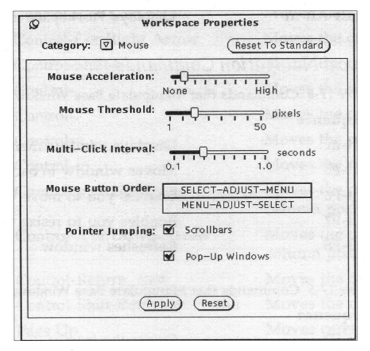

**Figure 2.59.** *Workspace properties for controlling mouse behavior*

## Microsoft Windows: Controlling Mouse Properties

Mouse characteristics in Microsoft Windows 95 and Windows NT are controlled through the Control Panel and double-clicking on the Mouse icon, which produces the window depicted in Figure 2.60. Mouse buttons, pointers, motion, and manufacturer type can be configured from this window.

The **Buttons** tab allows control of left- and right-handed mouse action and mouse speed. The test area is particularly amusing as a means of verifying the mouse settings. The **Pointers** tab lets you select a mouse pointer scheme. The pointer schemes are a collection of mouse pointer pictures that appears for various windows circumstances such as window sizing, double-clicking on an object, or using the left or right mouse buttons. Some of the schemes are animated. The **Pointer** tab lets you control pointer speed and trail. A pointer trail can be an effective visual aid when you move the mouse, to emphasize pointer direction. The **General** tab is where the mouse manufacturer is specified.

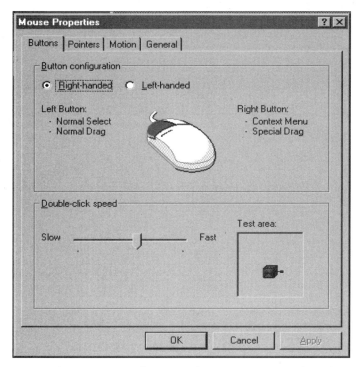

**Figure 2.60.** *Microsoft mouse characteristics control window*

# Chapter 3

# Building Programs and the Software Management Environment

U NIX and Windows both provide a variety of facilities to help develop, maintain, and manage software. Software management is also concerned with preserving program files and data and requires the use of backup or archiving facilities. This chapter will answer the following questions about managing, and building software in our environments:

- What facilities are available to control and record source-code changes?
- How do you create, compile, and build a program?
- What facilities are available for debugging programs?
- What backup facilities exist to preserve software?

## UNIX — Using the Source-Code Control System

The *Source-Code Control System* (SCCS) is a facility that allows source files to be maintained in a common library called a *version control library*. Source-code file removal and insertion relative to the library is controlled. Two people are prevented from accessing a file at the same time. A version control file contains the original file along with all the changes that have been applied to it. SCCS allows you to determine the status of any file and the name of the person who is currently using it. A complete history of changes and versions is maintained so that any version of the file may be retrieved. The term *delta* is used to refer to a version. The SCCS *delta ID* (SID) is composed of two fields, the release and the level. The initial delta for a file is 1.1, the second version is 1.2, and so on.

SCCS is actually a collection of several independent commands. The sccs command is the unified interface command and is usually invoked with another subcommand as follows:

```
sccs subcommand file
```

A history file for a source code program named myprog.c is established as follows:

```
mkdir SCCS
sccs create myprog.c
myprog.c:
1.1
20 lines
```

The mkdir command creates the sccs subdirectory. The sccs create command performs several functions, including renaming the original source program to myprog.c in the current directory, creating the history file s.myprog.c in the SCCS subdirectory, and performing an sccs get on myprog.c to retrieve a read-only copy of the initial version. SCCS is invoked to retrieve a file as follows:

```
sccs get program.c
```

This command retrieves a history file sccs/s.program.c. Various options can be specified with the get subcommand, some of which are:

-e    Retrieve a version for editing (same as edit command)
-k    Retrieve a writable copy but do not check out file
-m    Precede each line with the SCCS delta ID in which it was added

-cdate-time says to retrieve the latest version checked in prior to the date and time specified. -rsid says to retrieve the version corresponding to the SID specified. The -e option is used to check out a version of the file for editing by you. A p. form of the file is created in the sccs subdirectory. This file is now locked so that no one else can check this version in or out.

The SCCS delta command is utilized to check in a changed version of the file. The delta command only saves the differences between the old and new versions of the file. The effective ID must be the same as the user ID who checked out the file. The resulting delta of the new file version is the old delta number plus 1. The delta command also asks you to supply a comment describing the changes just made to the file before the file is finally returned. The SCCS delta command is invoked as follows:

```
sccs delta -s -y[comment]
```

The -s says not to report any delta information. The -y option specifies a comment affiliated with this change. If -y is omitted, the user is prompted for a comment. The info command displays the following information about a file:

- The version number checked out
- The version number to be checked in
- The name of the user who holds the lock
- The data and time the file was checked out

The info command is invoked as follows:

```
sccs info -b -u[username]
```

The -u option says to list only files checked out by this user. The -b option says to ignore branches. Branching results from requesting a previous version of a file. For example, a user may wish to check out an editable version 1.1 of a file. The system will not create a version 1.2

because that version already exists. Instead, a version 1.1.1.1 is created, followed by version 1.1.1.2 and so on. The `-b` command would ignore these versions.

## UNIX — Solaris and Linux — The `make` Utility

The `make` utility is a common means of building and maintaining programs in a UNIX environment. A `makefile` is required for the `make` utility to work properly. `Makefiles` are made up of a series of rules that describe how a program is to be compiled and linked. These rules can also indicate what kind of housekeeping, such as file purging, should be performed when running the `makefile`. The basic `makefile` includes the following rules and components:

### Target
The name of a file produced by a program, such as an executable or object file; can also be an action related to housecleaning.

### Dependencies
Specifies a file or files used as input to create the target.

### Command
Specifies an action carried out by the `make` utility. Several command lines may be required. Command lines must begin with a tab character.

The basic syntax for specifying these components is as follows:

```
target . . . : dependencies . . .
        command
        . . .
        . . .
```

A command represents a rule with dependencies. Usually the target will be built only if any if the dependencies change. This is not always the case, especially with respect to housecleaning rules, which may not rely on any dependencies. Command lines are distinguished from other lines in the `makefile` by the presence of a tab character at the beginning of the line. Figure 3.1 illustrates a simple `makefile`.

In Figure 3.1 the commands are the C compiler command lines cc -o and cc -c. The target files are the .o files. The dependencies are the .o files, the header (.h), files and the source files (.c). If a particular header file changes, or if a particular object file is missing, make must recompile that object file. If any of the object files change, or myprog does not exist, the executable myprog is rebuilt. There are no dependencies associated with the clean rule. The clean rule will only be invoked implicitly as make clean. What if make needs to build myprog with a file named clean? The clean rule must be rewritten as it appears in Figure 3.2.

```
myprog : main.o sort.o display.o calc.o printout.o

cc -o myprog main.o sort.o display.o calc.o printout.o

main.o : main.c mydefs.h
        cc -c main.c
sort.o : sort.c mydefs.h sort.h
        cc -c sort.c
display.o : display.c mydefs.h print.h
        cc -c display.c
calc.o : calc.c mydefs.h math.h
        cc -c calc.c
printout.o : printout.c mydefs print.h
        cc -c printout.c
clean :
        rm edit main.o sort.o display.o calc.o printout.o
```

**Figure 3.1.** *A basic* makefile

Variables can simplify makefiles. All of the object files from Figure 3.1 can be defined in the rule lines with the variable object as in Figure 3.2.

```
objects = main.o o sort.o display.o calc.o printout.o

myprog : $(objects)
         cc -o myprog $(objects)
       . . . .
.PHONY : clean
clean :
        -rm myprog $(objects)
```

**Figure 3.2.** makefile *rewritten with variables and modification to allow clean rule and a clean module*

Makefiles can be written in other styles, but Figures 3.1 and 3.2 depict the most popular forms. Furthermore, although makefiles are described under the UNIX category, make facilities (from gnu) also exist for the Microsoft Windows environment that work similarly to what we have just described.

## Microsoft Windows

Many software development and maintenance facilities exist for the Microsoft Windows environment. Borland C++ Version 5.0 is discussed in this chapter because that is what the author has for demonstration purposes. The Borland windows group appears as illustrated in Figure 3.3. Borland C++ utilizes the *Integrated Development Environment* (IDE), allowing you to write programs, debug them, compile, and browse through code and objects.

**Figure 3.3.** *The Borland C++ Version 5.0 window group*

Aside from the compiler itself (Borland C++), there are a variety of tools available for analyzing performance, debugging, and facilitating the building of sophisticated applications. The Turbo Debugger, Turbo Debugger Video Configuration, and Turbo Debugger Profiler are available for both the Windows and DOS environments. The WinSpector tool is used to perform a postmortem dump analysis of a Windows program experiencing a general protection fault. WinSight is a passive observer and is used to gather information about window classes and messages and application windows. The Turbo Profiler tools provide statistical information about where most of the time is spent in your application. The main Borland Version 5.0 C++ window is depicted in Figure 3.4.

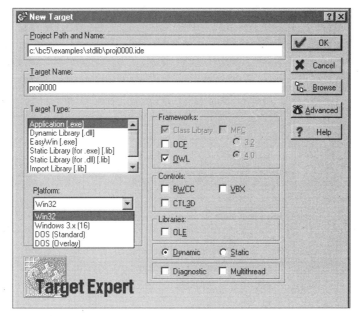

**Figure 3.4.** *Creating a new project with Borland C++*

Figure 3.4 illustrates the power of this utility, which actually prepares your program development environment based on choices you make in this window. Will the target be a non-overlayed DOS program or a 16-bit Windows application? If you are just building a simple C++ program and know the name of the file, upon invoking the C++ compiler, click on **Files** and click on the name of the file with which you want to work. In Figure 3.5, we have indicated that we wish to work on file `w32prime.c`. A vast number of utilities are at our disposal for working with this piece of code.

In Figure 3.5, the toolbar starting from the left and going to the right enables the following functionality: *Open a file, Save, Compile this file, Make a project, Build a project, Run (lightning bolt), Run to here, Statement step over, Statement step into, Pause process, Go to execution point, Toggle breakpoint, Undo, Cut, Copy, Paste, Search (flashlight), Search and replace, Search again, Browse a symbol, Split view horizontally, Split view vertically,* and *What's this?* A comprehensive discussion of every aspect of this facility is beyond the scope of this book.

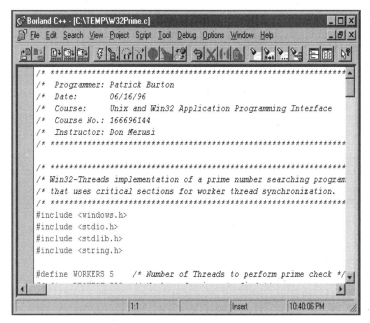

**Figure 3.5.** *A basic C++ program development window*

Projects in Borland C++ are like `makefiles` in UNIX. Notice that there is a **Make Project** and a **Build Project** choice on the toolbar. The **Make Project** button checks file dates and times to see if the target has been updated and should be incorporated into the build. The **Build Project** button causes all files to be rebuilt regardless of when they were updated last. The result of compiling this program is a real-time statistics screen during the compilation and a final statistics screen as depicted in Figure 3.6.

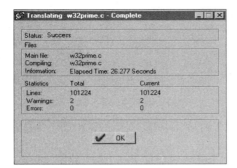

**Figure 3.6.** *Final stats screen for compiling* `w32prime.c`

# UNIX — File Backup with `tar`

The `tar` utility is available in both the Solaris and Linux environments for archiving or extracting files to or from a `tarfile`. A `tarfile` is a container file that can be written to disk or to a tape drive. Periodic `tar` backups can be scheduled by using the `cron` utility. The `tar` utility has a great many options, but only a few forms of it will be discussed here. The following command sequence copies all of the files from directory `thisdir` to directory `thatdir`:

```
cd thisdir; tar cf - . | (cd thatdir; tar fxp -)
```

The first `tar` command says to create a `tarfile` and send it to standard output (the `-`). The output is piped to the parenthesized command that changes to the directory where the `tarfile` will be unpacked. The second `tar` command says to extract the contents of the `tarfile` and restore the named files to their original modes and access control lists (ACLs) if appropriate. The following `tar` command creates an archive of the current directory to a tape mounted on drive `/dev/rmt/0`:

```
tar cvf /dev/rmt/0
```

The contents of a `tarfile` can be displayed by using the following command:

```
tar tvf /dev/rmt/0
```

This command will display the contents of the `tarfile` written to tape drive `/dev/rmt/0`.

To save space, it is customary to compress `tarfiles` with such utilities as `compress` or GNU ZIP (`gzip`). A compressed tarfile's file name is appended with a `.z` or a `.gz`.

## Microsoft Windows Backup

Both Windows NT and Windows 95 have a backup facility. By clicking on the **My Computer** shortcut on the desktop, clicking once on the disk drive of interest, then clicking with the right mouse button and choosing **Properties**, you will get the screen shown in Figure 3.7.

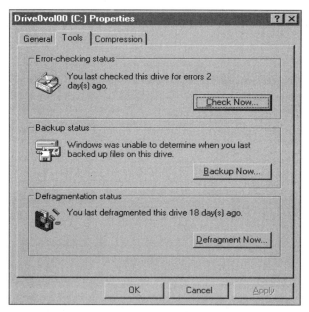

**Figure 3.7.** *The Tools tab from the disk drive properties menu*

The backup utility is invoked from here. Selecting **Backup Now...** brings up the display in Figure 3.8. This utility is self-explanatory. It performs backups and restores to and from all the devices it discovers on your system. The backups and restores can be performed in a variety of ways. In Figure 3:9, the **Options** frame is displayed and the **Backup** tab was selected.

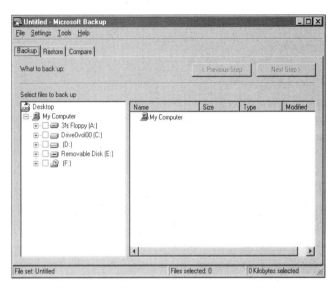

**Figure 3.8.** *Main backup screen in Microsoft windows*

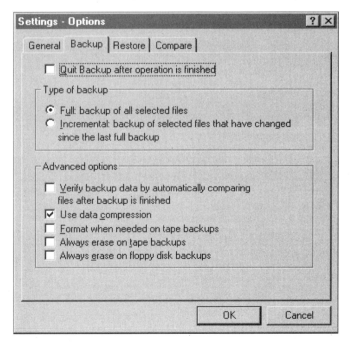

**Figure 3.9.** *Microsoft Windows Backup options screen*

Many options are available for controlling how backup should be performed, such as whether all files should be backed up or just the files that have changed (incremental backup).

## Debugging Facilities in OpenWindows

The debugging facility in Solaris and Linux works on both a tty screen and an OpenWindows terminal. The OpenWindows version is called `debugger` and the tty version is called `dbx`. Programs are compiled with option `-g` to incorporate the debugger during execution. These utilities are source-level debuggers for ANSI C, C++, Pascal, and FORTRAN programs. The `debugger` utility accepts the same commands as `dbx`, but provides a convenient, graphical user interface and uses `dbx` for all debugging functionality. The debugger utility allows you to use the mouse to set breakpoints, examine the values of variables, control execution, browse source files, and so on. The debugger utility has separate windows for viewing source code, entering commands, monitoring expressions, setting properties, and other uses.

## The GNU Debugger

Another convenient debugging facility for the UNIX and MS-DOS environments (and for the DOS window in Windows NT and 95) comes from the GNU organization and works seamlessly with the infamous `emacs` editor. The `gdb` debugger can be invoked from within an `emacs` session and produces a full-screen source-level debugging screen. Using the appropriate key strokes, you can easily flip back and forth between an editing and compile–debug session. Programs are compiled with the `-g` (debug option) option to allow interaction with `gdb`. Figure 3.10 illustrates an `emacs-gdb` session.

`gdb` commands are entered in the top window and the command results are displayed in the lower window. The `=>` in the lower window indicates the current source line at which the program is going to execute. `gdb` allows the user to establish breakpoints at different lines and to examine the contents of program variables.

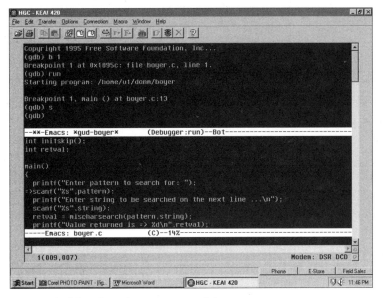

**Figure 3.10.** *Sample* `emacs-gdb` *debug session*

# Chapter 4

# The Win32 API and
# UNIX System Services

The Win32 Application Program Interface provides an extremely comprehensive collection of routines to perform a wealth of system operations from a program. Because of the huge scope of the Win32 API, this chapter will focus on specific features and contrast them with what is available in Solaris and Linux. The specific routines to be contrasted are involved in the following kinds of operations: process and thread scheduling, synchronization and concurrency control, memory management, and file operations. This chapter answers the following questions:

- What is the difference between a process and a thread?
- How do you create processes and threads?
- What is the scheduling criteria for processes and threads?
- How are processes and threads synchronized?
- What concurrency and synchronization primitives exist on the system?
- How can a process or thread control the amount of memory it utilizes?
- How can a process or thread perform file I/O?
- What kinds of file I/O can be performed?
- How can memory space be allocated and deallocated?
- How can memory be shared?
- How are pipes created and used?

## Process and Thread Scheduling

Both UNIX and Microsoft Windows provide a means of scheduling other processes and threads. A process may consist of one or more threads of execution. A complex process may have several threads of concurrent execution. Threads programming is a more efficient way of performing multitasked types of operations because the context switch between threads is much more streamlined than it is between processes. Think of threads as "subroutines" that can execute independently of the rest of the program, but share the same area of memory and context. A multithreaded program could have one thread waiting for terminal input, another thread printing a report, and still another thread performing a sort on some data in a disk file. All of these functions would take place simultaneously. In Solaris and Linux, pthread calls are available for creating and managing threads. Solaris also has the *Light-Weight Process* (LWP) library, which can be used to create and manage threads, along with a variety of communication and synchronization functions. For Windows 95 and Windows NT, the Win32 API provides the routines necessary for creating processes and threads.

## UNIX — Process and Thread Creation in Solaris and Linux Using pthread Calls

The pthread interface is based on Draft 4 of the proposed IEEE standards for multithreaded programming, POSIX 1003.4a. Both the Solaris and the Linux versions of UNIX support these calls. The following basic routines are used to create, manage and destroy threads in both the Solaris and the Linux environments. The repertoire of pthread calls is extensive, and a comprehensive discussion of every routine is beyond the scope of this book.

### *Starting a Thread:*

```
pthread_create (
        thread_id,      /* Id of created thread */
        thread_attrs,   /* Set to pthread_attr_default */
        entry_point,    /* Thread routine */
        thread_arg );   /* Optional argument to pass */
```

### Terminating a Thread:

```
pthread_exit (
    *status);   /* Exit status of thread */
```

### Waiting for a Thread to Terminate:

```
pthread_join (
        thread_id,    /* Id of thread to wait for */
        *status );    /* Status of terminating thread */
```

### Deleting a Thread:

```
pthread_detach (
        thread_id );  /* Id of thread marked for deletion */
```

The call to `pthread_join` is similar to a call to the Solaris LWP routine `thr_join`. Any number of threads can successfully call `pthread_join` and be awakened when the thread specified by `thread_id` terminates.

Threads created with the `pthread` calls can be scheduled according to three different policies, *FIFO, round-robin,* and *default.* These policy settings are accomplished with a call to `pthread_attr_set sched`. `Pthread` threads can also be scheduled with various priorities. These priorities are described as minimum and maximum and occur for each of the scheduling policies previously mentioned. The priority settings are accomplished with a call to `pthread_attr_setprio`.

*Process* creation is performed by using the `exec` and `fork` functions, which are typically used together. Function `fork` works in a very interesting way, and no comparable routine exists in the Win32 environment. When a call is made to `fork`, a complete replica of the original process is created. In the replica, execution begins *at the point of the* `fork` *call.* A return code of zero indicates that the `fork` call was done in the replica and not the original process. By evaluating the status returned from the `fork` call, we can make a decision based on whether we are executing in the original process or the replicated process. If we are in the replicated process, a call is made to the `exec` function. The `exec` function comes in several forms, depending on how arguments to it are passed. The basic argument passed to the `exec` function is the name of the program to load into memory. The program is loaded right over the top of the program making the `exec` call, which happens to be the replicated program. This is a classic UNIX way of running one program from another program. The following code sequence demonstrates the use of `fork` and `exec`.

```
if (fork() == 0)         /* If true then in replica */
    execlp("newprog", "newprog", (char *) 0);
```

In this code sequence, the `exec` function requests that program `newprog` be executed. The process making this call is replaced by process `newprog`. The arguments to `exec` consist of the name of the program file and the command required to activate the program. The `lp` form of the `exec` call means the argument list is terminated by a zero character.

Another variation of the `fork` call is `vfork`. Function `vfork` does not make a complete replica of the original program, but attempts to use the original copy as a `fork`ed copy to save memory. The use of `fork` routines with threads creates a curious predicament. If a multi-threaded process performs a `fork` operation, are all the threads replicated? Indeed they are! This is usually not the desired effect, and a call to `fork1` is performed that creates only the primary thread of execution to be continued in the replica.

## UNIX — Thread Creation and Management in Solaris Using the Light-Weight Process Library

The Light-Weight Process (LWP) library in Solaris offers several other options for working with threads. Although threads themselves are sometimes referred to as LWPs, the term in this context refers more to the execution resource recognized by Solaris. Every executing thread is assigned to an LWP. The number of LWPs is limited and can have a behavioral effect on the execution of a multithreaded process. More LWPs can be requested either by making a call specifically to request more LWPs or as part of the LWP thread-creation function. The LWP thread-creation routine is as follows:

```
thr_create (
    void *stackbase,          // Default = NULL
    size_t stacksize,         // Default = NULL
    void *(*startfcn)(void *), // Thread entry point
    void *param,              // NULL = no arguments
    long flags,               // Flags
    thread_t *threadID);      // Will receive identifier
```

The calling argument flags can be set to THR_NEW_LWP, ensuring the availability of an LWP resource for this thread. The *thread ID* is a unique number associated with this thread. The thread ID is used in all subsequent LWP routines related to thread control and management. The following LWP routines can be used to suspend and resume a thread:

```
thr_suspend(thread_t threadID);

thr_continue(thread_t threadID);
```

The following routine can be used to increase the number of LWPs available:

```
thr_setconcurrency ( int new_level );
```

The argument new_level refers to how many LWP resource units should be established. This argument can be set to zero, in which case the system allocates just enough LWPs to keep the process going. Routine thr_join is used to wait for a particular thread to terminate.

```
thr_join(
    thread_t wait_for,
    thread_t departed,
    void **status);
```

Routine thr_join will wait for the thread specified in the first argument. If the call is successful, the second argument will contain the identifier of the terminated thread. If a zero is specified for the first argument, thr_join will acknowledge the first thread to terminate. Only one thread can successfully perform the thr_join. Any other thread performing a thr_join after the first successful call will receive an error.

## Process and Thread Creation and Management Using the Win32 API

Process and thread creation using the Win32 API involves routines CreateProcess, CreateThread, WaitForSingleObject, and WaitForMultipleObjects. The WaitFor routines are actually involved for synchronization reasons with many other objects that can exist in a Windows 95 or Windows NT system, such as semaphores, mutexes, files, and events. These objects are discussed in a later section of this chapter.

The calling sequence to CreateProcess is as follows:

```
Handle = CreateProcess(
    Image,                  /* Program file to run */
    Command,                /* Command to invoke program */
    Process_Sec_Attr,       /* Process security */
    Thread_Sec_Attr,        /* Primary thread security */
    InheritFlag,            /* Controls handle inheritance */
    CreationMode,           /* How process is created */
    Environment,            /* Environmental variables */
    CurrentDir,             /* Current directory */
    StartupInfo,            /* Startup information structure */
    ProcessInfo );          /* Process/primary thread info */
```

A *handle* is a unique data value returned from most Win32 object-creation routines. A handle represents the object to the system. The two security attributes arguments in this API call, Process_Sec_Attr, and Thread_Sec_Attr, describe a security structure used only in the Windows NT environment. NT provides a robust security environment that will be discussed in a later section of this chapter. Many Win32 API routines contain a security attributes argument. The InheritFlag argument is boolean and controls whether the handle resulting from the creation of this process can be passed to another process or thread. The CreationMode argument controls how the process is created, such as suspended or in debug mode. The Environment argument describes any environmental variables such as those symbols initialized by the SET command in the MS-DOS command procedures. Argument CurrentDir indicates the current directory from which the process will run. The last two arguments, StartupInfo and ProcessInfo, decribe structures. The StartupInfo structure is extensive and consists of the following items:

```
structure StartupInfo {
  DWORD cb;                 /* Size of this structure */
  LPSTR lpReserved;         /* Set to NULL */
  LPSTR lpDesktop;          /* Desk top object, set to NULL */
  LPSTR lpTitle;            /* The console title bar */
  DWORD dwX;                /* Coordinates of upper-left corner */
  DWORD dwY;                /* ... of this window */
  DWORD dwXSize;            /* Window width */
  DWORD dwYSize;            /* Window height */
  DWORD dwXCountChars;      /* Console window width */
  DWORD dwYCountChars;      /* Console window height */
  DWORD dwFillAttribute;    /* Console text, backgrnd colors */
```

```
  DWORD dwFlags;       /* What fields in this structure to activate */
  WORD wShowWindow;    /* How applications first window should appear */
  WORD cbReserved2;    /* Set to zero */
  WORD lpReserved2;    /* Set to NULL */
  HANDLE hStdInput;    /* Handle for standard input */
  HANDLE hStdOutput;   /* Handle for standard output */
  HANDLE hStdError;    /* Handle for standard error output */
}
```

It is only necessary to initialize the first element of this data structure. The `ProcessInfo` structure contains information returned by the system.

```
struct _PROCESS_INFORMATION {
  HANDLE hProcess;   /* Created process handle */
  HANDLE hThread;    /* Created thread handle */
  DWORD dwProcessId; /* Created process id */
  DWORD dwThreadId;  /* Created thread id */
} ProcessInfo;
```

A thread is created with routine `CreateThread` as follows:

```
CreateThread (
  Security,       /* Security attributes */
  Stack,          /* Thread local stack */
  Routine,        /* Routine entry point */
  Tparm,          /* Arguments passed to thread */
  CreateMode,     /* How thread is created */
  ThreadID);      /* Id associated with thread */
```

The `WaitFor` routines will be introduced here, although they have ramifications beyond processes and threads. These routines can be used to coordinate waiting for a single process or thread, or for many processes or threads, to terminate. The routines have the following calling sequence:

```
Status = WaitForSingleObject (
  HANDLE Object,           /* Object Handle for which to wait */
  DWORD Timeout );         /* Set to INFINITE or timeout value */

Status = WaitForMultipleObjects (
  DWORD Objects,      /* Number of objects to check */
  LPHANDLE Handles,   /* Array of handles of objects */
  BOOL Waitflag,      /* Wait for 1 or all objects */
  DWORD Timeout );    /* Set to INFINITE or timeout value */
```

The `Handles` arguments in the `WaitFor` routines can represent other object handles for which synchronization can be performed.

Threads can be resumed and suspended by using the following Win32 routines:

```
Status = ResumeThread ( HANDLE Object );

Status = SuspendThread ( HANDLE Object );
```

Win32 thread priorities range from 1 to 31. The system gives more time to higher-priority threads. Threads running at the same priority execute in a round-robin style. Win32 threads can be scheduled according to four priority classes:

| Class | CreateMode argument | Priority level |
|---|---|---|
| Real time | REAL_TIME_PRIORITY_CLASS | 24 |
| High | HIGH_PRIORITY_CLASS | 13 |
| Normal | NORMAL_PRIORITY_CLASS | 9/7 |
| Idle | IDLE_PRIORITY_CLASS | 4 |

These values are defined by the environment and are specified in the `CreateMode` argument of the `CreateProcess` or `CreateThread` calls. The two priority levels for the normal class represent programs running in the foreground (9) and background (7). Specific Win32 thread priorities can be adjusted even further by using routine `SetThreadPriority`. This routine can adjust the thread priority from –2 to +2 around the process priority. A specific thread priority can also be set to a time-critical level of 15.

## UNIX — Process and Thread Synchronization in Solaris and Linux Using Semaphores

Semaphore operations can be described as the following mathematical functions wait(s) and signal(s) where s is a semaphore variable.

```
WAIT(S):
    If S # 0 then wait here;
           else
        S <= S - 1;
        Enter critical section;

    SIGNAL(S):
        S = S + 1;
```

The semaphore variable s can be initialized to any *nonzero* value. Three routines are involved in creating, detecting, and managing semaphores. Semaphores are created by calling routine `semget` as follows:

```
semid = semget ( key, number_of_sems, flags );
```

Argument key is usually set to IPC_PRIVATE. A set of semaphores can actually be created with this call by specifying the number desired in the second argument, number_of_sems. The last argument, flags, usually specifies protection, along with a creation mode, which is typically IPC_CREAT.

Once a semaphore set has been created and an identifier (semid) is passed back from the call to semget, specific operations on the semaphores can be performed with a call to routine semctl as follows:

```
semctl ( semid, semvar, operation, oper_val );
```

The first argument is the identifier obtained from having called semget. The next argument, semvar, is a variable name chosen by the caller representing the semaphore variable. Argument operation specifies such actions as whether we are setting the semaphore to a certain value or reading what value at which the semaphore is set. The last argument will contain the current value of the semaphore if the caller is performing a read operation (GETVAL) or the value to which the semaphore will be set if the caller is performing a write operation (SETVAL). This routine can also be used to remove a semaphore set from the system by specifying IPC_RMID for the operation argument. Actions performed by a call to semctl always complete. To appreciate the effect of a semaphore, routine semop is called as follows:

```
semop ( semid, sops, n_sops );
```

This routine will perform n_sops operations defined in sops on a particular semaphore set. Argument sops actually represents a structure describing what semaphore is to be accessed and what kind of action is to be performed:

```
struct sembuf semset;
....
semset.sem_num;    /* Semaphore number */
semset.sem_op;     /* Operation, e.g., -1 or +1 */
semset.sem_flg;    /* Operation flags */
```

A WAIT(S) operation can be accomplished by using the following code, assuming we have already called routine semget and have the semaphore ID semid:

```
struct sembuf semset;
....
semset.sem_num = 0;
semset.sem_op = -1;
semset.sem_flg = 0;
....
if(semop(semid, &semset, 1) == -1)perror("semop error");
....
```

The `SIGNAL(S)` function is performed in almost exactly the same way,
except the `semset.sem_op` is set to a +1.

## UNIX — Process and Thread Synchronization in Solaris and Linux Using `pthread` Routines

The `pthread` routine library provides three mechanisms for enforcing
synchronization: *global locks, mutexes,* and *condition variables.* The
`pthread` global lock is actually a special kind of mutex. Mutexes are
synchronization primitives that work by becoming owned by a
thread. Once a mutex is owned or locked, any other threads that
attempt to lock the mutex are made to wait. When a mutex is
unlocked, any thread waiting to acquire ownership will be granted
the mutex. Condition variables are like signals. If a thread is not waiting for a condition variable when it is signaled, the signal has no
effect. Condition variables are used in conjunction with mutexes to
enforce mutual exclusion. It is assumed that you are familiar with the
concept of mutual exclusion and the critical section. Mutexes are
locked by threads before they enter their critical sections. Within the
critical section, the thread determines the validity of the data for
which it is processing. If the data is determined to be valid, it is
processed and the mutex is unlocked. If the data is not valid, the
thread waits for the conditional variable to be signaled. The call
involved in performing this operation also involves automatically
unlocking the mutex. The mutex is unlocked to allow other threads
to access the critical section. Once the condition variable is signaled,
the thread locks the mutex again and attempts to determine if the
data is valid. The condition variable signaling is referred to as broad-
casting in the calls. The `pthread` call for locking and unlocking the
global mutex is performed as follows:

```
pthread_lock_global_np();
pthread_unlock_global_np();
```

The mutex calls are as follows:

```
pthread_mutex_init (              /* Create the mutex */
    pthread_mutex_t *mutex,       /* Mutex identifier */
    pthread_mutexattr_t attr);    /* Mutex attributes */

pthread_mutex_lock (              /* Lock mutex */
    pthread_mutex_t *mutex );

pthread_mutex_unlock (            /* Unlock mutex */
    pthread_mutex_t *mutex );

pthread_mutex_destroy (           /* Delete mutex */
    pthread_mutex_t *mutex );

pthread_mutex_trylock (           /* Check if mutex */
    pthread_mutex_t *mutex );     /* can be locked */
```

The condition variable calls are as follows:

```
pthread_cond_init (              /* Create CV */
    pthread_cond_t *cond,        /* CV identifier */
    pthread_condattr_t attr );   /* CV attributes */

pthread_cond_broadcast (        /* Wake all threads */
    pthread_cond_t *cond );     /* waiting for CV */

pthread_cond_destroy (          /* Delete CV */
    pthread_cond_t *cond );

pthread_cond_signal (           /* Wake one thread */
    pthread_cond_t *cond );     /* waiting for this CV */

pthread_cond_wait (             /* Wait for CV to be */
    pthread_cond_t *cond );     /* signaled or broadcast */

pthread_cond_timedwait (        /* Wait for CV to be */
    pthread_cond_t *cond );     /* signaled or broadcast for
                                   time specified */
```

## UNIX — Process and Thread Creation and Synchronization in Solaris Using the Light-Weight Process Library

The Solaris Light-Weight Process Library provides a means of creating and managing threads, as well as many other functions that are beyond the scope of this book. The LWP calls nearly all have equivalent pthread calls; however, some of the routine arguments and their implications differ. Thread creation in Solaris using these routines involves a system resource called a light-weight process. The execution of a thread is *conveyed* by means of an LWP. When you log into Solaris, a pool of LWPs is made available to your environment. When required, the system obtains an LWP resource from this pool, and they can be ultimately exhausted. However, one of the arguments that can be specified to the LWP thread-creation routine allows an LWP to be created with the thread, rather than having the system use an LWP from the pool. The routine used to create a thread is thr_create and is called as follows:

```
thr_create (
    void *stackbase,            /* Default = NULL */
    size_t stacksize,           /* Default = NULL */
    void *(*startfcn)(void *),  /* Thread entry point */
    void *param,                /* NULL = no arguments */
    long flags,                 /* Flags */
    thread_t *threadID);        /* Will receive identifier */
```

The caller has the option of specifying the thread local stack address and stack size. The **flags** argument can be set to the following values:

| | |
|---|---|
| THR_NEW_LWP | Guarantees an LWP resource will be available for this thread |
| THR_SUSPENDED | Thread is created suspended |
| THR_DAEMON | thr_join will not wait for a daemon thread |

Two different routines can be used to wait for threads, thr_join and thr_wait. These routines are used to ensure that threads are not prematurely terminated. The calling sequences to these routines are as follows:

```
thr_join (
    thread_t *threadID,      /* Thread ID to wait for */
    thread_t *depthreadID,   /* Departed thread id */
    long status );           /* Departed thread status */

thr_wait ( thread_t *threadID );
```

Solaris LWP threads can be suspended and resumed as follows:

```
thr_suspend ( thread_t threadID );

thr_continue ( thread_t threadID );
```

The Solaris LWP library provides four synchronization control mechanisms: *mutexes, condition variables, read/write locks,* and *semaphores.* The mutexes and condition variables function similarly to the pthread versions. The read/write locks are designed for use in a database environment where read/write access to disk file data is to be controlled. For instance, you may want to allow only one thread to have write capability, but allow any number of threads to have the ability to read. The calling sequences to the mutex routines are as follows:

```
mutex_init (             /* Mutex creation */
    mutex_t muxptr,      /* Mutex identifier */
    int muxtype,         /* Mutex scope type */
    int param );         /* Optional characteristics */


mutex_lock (             /* Lock mutex */
    mutex_t *muxptr);


mutex_unlock (           /* Unlock mutex */
    mutex_t *muxptr);


mutex_destroy (          /* Delete mutex */
    mutex_t *muxptr);


mutex_trylock (          /* Test if mutex can be locked */
    mutex_t *muxptr);
```

The calling sequence to the condition variable routines are as follows:

```
cond_init (              /* Create condition variable */
    cond_t *condvar,     /* CV identifier */
    int condtyp,         /* CV scope type */
    int param );         /* Optional characteristics */


cond_destroy (           /* Delete CV */
    cond_t *condvar);


cond_wait (              /* Wait for CV signal */
    cond_t *condvar,
    mutex_t *muxptr);


cond_signal (            /* Signal one thread */
    cond_t *condvar);

cond_broadcast (         /* Signal all threads */
    cond_t *condvar);
```

```
cond_timedwait (           /* Wait for specified */
   cond_t *condvar,        /* time period for CV */
   mutex_t *muxptr,
   timestruct_t *timeabs);
```

The read/write routines have the following calling sequence:

```
rwlock_init (              /* Create r/w lock */
   rwlock_t *rwlockp,      /* R/W lock id */
   int rwlocktyp,          /* Scope type */
   void * param );         /* Optional characteristics */


rwlock_destroy (           /* Delete r/w lock */
   rwlock_t *rwlockp);


rw_wrlock (                /* Request write lock */
   rwlock_t *rwlockp);


rw_rdlock (                /* Request read lock */
   rwlock_t *rwlockp);


rw_trywrlock (             /* Try to get a write lock */
   rwlock_t *rwlockp);


rw_tryrdlock (             /* Try to get a read lock */
   rwlock_t *rwlockp);
```

The LWP semaphore routines perform the classic WAIT(S)/SIGNAL(S) semaphore operations and have the following calling sequence:

```
sema_init (                       /* Create semaphore */
   sema_t *semaphore,             /* Semaphore ID */
   unsigned int sema_cnt,         /* Initialize count */
   int sematype,                  /* Scope of semaphore */
   int param )                    /* Opt. characteristics */

sema_destroy (                    /* Delete semaphore */
   sema_t *semaphore );


sema_wait (                       /* Block on semaphore */
   sema_t *semaphore );           /* until count > 0 */


sema_trywait (                    /* Decrements count if */
   sema_t *semaphore );           /* semaphore cnt = 0 */


sema_post (                       /* Increment semaphore */
   sema_t *semaphore );           /* count */
```

The calling argument pattern is similar in all of these LWP routines. The *type* argument that appears in the _init calls determines the scope of impact of the synchronization as process-wide (USYNC_PROCESS) or thread-wide (USYNC_THREAD). The _try versions of these routines are interesting because they let you test the condition before actually committing to it.

## UNIX — Memory Management Allocation/Deallocation Routines in Solaris and Linux

The C ANSI standard routines are available in both Solaris and Linux. These routines include the basic collection of calls that can be used to allocate and deallocate memory as required. The calling sequences are as follows:

***Pass back address pointing to*** size ***bytes of memory:***
```
void *malloc(size_t size);
```

***Pass back address pointing to*** number size ***byte segments of memory:***
```
void *calloc(size_t number, size_t size);
```

***Change size of allocated area of memory pointed to by*** ptr ***to*** size
```
void *realloc(void *ptr, size_t size);
```

***Free memory segment pointed to by*** ptr ***(use with*** calloc***):***
```
int cfree(void *ptr);
```

***Free memory segment pointed to by*** ptr ***(use with*** malloc***):***
```
int free(void *ptr);
```

## UNIX — Shared Memory Routines in Solaris and Linux

The shared memory routines are part of the IPC family of functions. Three routines are involved, and they have the following calling sequence:

### Create a shared memory segment ID:

```
semid = shmget (
    key,          /* Unique identifier value */
    bytes,        /* Size of shared area */
    flags);       /* Ownership and protection */
```

### Pass back address pointer to shared memory segment:

```
ptr = shmat (
    semid,     /* From shmget call */
    address,   /* Address of shared segment */
    flags);    /* Option flags */
```

### Perform operations on shared memory segment (usually to remove it):

```
shmctl (
    semid,     /* From shmget call */
    command,   /* Typically IPC_RMID, remove */
    status);   /* Status buffer */
```

Housekeeping is important when using the IPC routines. Failure to call shmctl when a process terminates results in the memory segment being left behind. If enough of these memory segments accumulate, the resulting condition can compromise system operation. It is possible to use the shell command IPCRM to remove the segments; however, it is better to call shmctl with the command IPC_RMID.

# UNIX — Pipes in Solaris and Linux

Pipes act as virtual I/O devices that allow data transfer between two or more threads without involving I/O. There are two varieties of pipes in UNIX, *unnamed* and *named*. The behavior of these two types of pipes is characteristically very different. Routine pipe is used to create an unnamed pipe as follows:

```
pipe ( fd );
```

Routine pipe returns two file descriptors: fd[0] is for reading and fd[1] is for writing. Information flow in an unnamed pipe is unidirectional. Unnamed pipes are only available within the context of the creating process and any of its children. Two unnamed pipes must be created to perform full-duplex data transfer. An attempt to write on the pipe whose other end has been closed results in a *broken pipe* message.

Named pipes are considered special files called FIFOs and are created using the `mknod` call as follows:

```
mknod   ("PipeName", S_FIFO, 0);
```

This call would create a named pipe called `PipeName`. Named pipes are available system-wide. Processes interact with the named pipe by specifying the name as a file name in an open function call and using the conventional file I/O functions such as `read`, `write`, and `close`. Named pipes also transfer information in one direction only. The behavior of named pipes can be controlled by specifying a bit as part of the open call. The bit `O_NDELAY` determines how the pipe is to react depending on circumstances at the different ends of the pipe. For example, if the pipe action is to open for read, but the far end is not opened for write and the `O_NDELAY` is specified, the open succeeds. If the `O_NDELAY` is not specified, the process waits to read until the far end is opened for write.

## Win32 API — Process and Thread Synchronization

The synchronization primitives in the Win32 API are valid for both Windows 95 and Windows NT. The security attributes structure found in these calls is valid only for the NT environment. As stated earlier, synchronization can be determined from more than just synchronization objects. This chapter will focus on *mutexes, semaphores, events,* and *critical sections;* however, the following table indicates how synchronization can be determined from other Win32 objects. The idea of an object being signaled or unsignaled is important to understanding how a Win32 object indicates synchronization.

| *Object* | *When considered signaled .....* |
|---|---|
| *event* | Set exclusively with SetEvent or PulseEvent function |
| *mutex* | When not owned by a thread |
| *semaphore* | When semaphore variable count is > 0 |
| *process* | Final thread terminates |
| *thread* | Thread terminates |
| *timer* | Timer expires |
| *file* | File I/O operation finishes |

Win32 mutexes are created and manipulated with routines
CreateMutex, OpenMutex, and ReleaseMutex. Mutexes are created by calling routine CreateMutex as follows:

```
Handle = CreateMutex (
        LPSECURITY_ATTRIBUTES SecAttrib,
        BOOL Owner,
        LPSTR MutexName );
```

The security attributes argument SecAttrib describes a security structure. In Windows NT, this structure can be set up to control who can
access the mutex and what actions they can perform. If no security is
required to establish the mutex, a NULL is passed for this argument. The
Owner argument can be set to true or false to indicate whether this mutex
should be owned immediately upon being created. Once a mutex is
owned, other threads that attempt to acquire it are made to wait. The
last argument, MutexName, indicates the name associated with this mutex.
A cousin call to CreateMutex is OpenMutex, which assumes the mutex has
already been created. The caller need only specify the mutex name to
the OpenMutex call, which has the following calling sequence:

```
Handle = OpenMutex (
        DWORD Access,
        BOOL Inheritance,
        LPTSTR MutexName );
```

The **Access** argument can be set to SYNCHRONIZE or MUTEX_ALL_ACCESS
and has implications for how a mutex handle is managed in subsequent wait calls. The **Inheritance** argument controls whether this
mutex handle can be passed to other processes or threads. A mutex is
given up by using the ReleaseMutex routine, which has the following
calling sequence:

```
ReleaseMutex ( mHandle mutex );
```

A thread or process waits for the mutex to become available by using
routine WaitForSingleObject. The wait for the mutex to become signaled can lead to some different end results. The mutex wait could
end successfully, or it could end with an indication that the mutex has
been *abandoned*—the mutex has been deleted from the system and
the outcome of the wait-for call should be questioned.

The Win32 semaphore functions involve the following three API routines: CreateSemaphore, OpenSemaphore, and ReleaseSemaphore. Routine CreateSemaphore has the following calling sequence:

```
Handle = CreateSemaphore (
        LPSECURITY_ATTRIBUTE SecAttrib,
        LONG InitCount,
        LONG MaxRefCount,
        LPTSTR SemaName );
```

The security attributes argument can be specified to control access to a semaphore; otherwise this argument is set to NULL. The next two arguments, InitCount and MaxRefCount, are used to establish the initial semaphore count and the maximum number of references that can be made to this semaphore, respectively. The semaphore name is indicated in the last argument. Routine OpenSemaphore can be used to affiliate with a semaphore that has already been established. The arguments associated with this call are identical to those of the OpenMutex.

```
Handle = OpenSemaphore (
        DWORD Access,
        BOOL Inheritance,
        LPTSTR SemaName );
```

A Win32 call, ReleaseSemaphore, is available to change the value of a semaphore at any time. This routine has the following calling sequence:

```
BOOL ReleaseSemaphore (
        HANDLE Semaphore,
        LONG CountChange,
        LPLONG RememberCount );
```

Argument CountChange represents the amount by which the current semaphore count will be *incremented*. The caller can preserve the semaphore count *before* the effect of CountChange occurs by specifying argument RememberCount. There is no wait-for-semaphore call specifically; this function is accomplished with the routine WaitForSingleObject, specifying the handle of the semaphore as the first argument. The effect of a SIGNAL(S) is attained with the ReleaseSemaphore routine.

Another Win32 synchronization object, the *event*, is used to indicate the occurrence of an incident rather than to control access to a shared resource. Events are created with the following routine:

```
Handle = CreateEvent (
        LPSECURITY_ATTRIBUTES SecAttrib,
        BOOL ManualReset,
        BOOL InitialState,
        LPTSTR EventName );
```

Events can be controlled manually or automatically. Argument `ManualReset` indicates whether it is desired to have the system automatically reset an event to nonsignaled after a wait-for function or to let the caller explicitly perform the reset action. An event can also be created as signaled or nonsignaled, according to whether the argument `InitialState` is set to true or false. This can be convenient for satisfying a wait-for condition upon initially creating an event. The last argument is where the name of the event object is specified. Other event object routines are as follows:

```
Handle = OpenEvent (
        DWORD Access,
        BOOL Inheritance,
        LPTSTR EventName );


BOOL SetEvent ( HANDLE Event );


BOOL ResetEvent ( HANDLE Event );


BOOL PulseEvent ( HANDLE Event );
```

The `PulseEvent` routine performs a `SetEvent/ResetEvent` in one call.

The next synchronization facility, the *critical section*, is only effective within a single process and not system-wide. Three routines are involved when using critical sections:

```
InitializeCriticalSection
EnterCriticalSection
LeaveCriticalSection.
```

A critical section structure must also be established as follows:

```
CRITICAL_SECTION YourCriticalSection;
```

This structure is specified in all subsequent critical section calls:

```
....
InitializeCriticalSection(&YourCriticalSection);
....
EnterCriticalSection(&YourCriticalSection);
....
LeaveCriticalSection(&YourCriticalSection);
....
```

## Microsoft Windows — Memory Management Routines

Several different memory management facilities exist as part of the Windows NT and Windows 95 environments. The ANSI standard C calls, such as `malloc`, `free`, and `realloc`, are available as part of supplemental programming packages that can be installed in these environments. These routines can be found in such programming packages as Borland's C/C++ and Microsoft's Visual C/C++.

The Win32 API provides two facilities, *heap routines* and *virtual memory routines*. The heap routines are more of an historical carryover from 16-bit Windows. This book does not attempt to discuss the differences between 16-bit and 32-bit Windows programming. Seven heap routines are provided as follows:

| | |
|---|---|
| HeapCreate | Create heap, handle of heap is returned; used in all subsequent calls |
| HeapAlloc | Allocate memory from heap |
| HeapReAlloc | Change size of heap |
| HeapSize | Retrieve size of heap |
| HeapFree | Release memory block within heap |
| HeapDestroy | Entire heap is eliminated |
| GetProcessHeap | Get handle of default heap created at birth of process |

Routine HeapCreate is called as follows:

```
HHandle = HeapCreate (
    DWORD Flags,        /* How is heap created */
    DWORD HeapSize,     /* How many bytes is heap */
    DWORD MaxSize);     /* How big can heap get */
```

The `Flags` argument in `HeapCreate` can control concurrent access to the heap. It is recommended that `HEAP_NO_SERIALIZE` be specified to control two threads attempting to allocate memory simultaneously from the heap. Once the heap is created, memory must specifically be allocated from the heap by calling routine HeapAlloc as follows:

```
HeapAlloc (
    HANDLE HHandle,      /* Handle from HeapCreate */
    DWORD Flags,         /* Allocation flags */
    DWORD AllocSize);    /* How much memory allocated */
```

The Flags argument in HeapAlloc is handy for specifying such arguments as HEAP_ZERO_MEMORY, which writes zeroes into the allocated area of memory.

The Win32 API also provides a set of virtual-memory management routines, VirtualAlloc and VirtualFree. The concept of *reserving* versus *committing* memory must be understood before these routines can be used effectively. When memory is reserved, it is not physically allocated to the process. Any attempt to reference reserved memory results in an invalid address exception. Reserved memory is not accounted for in the system paging file. When memory is committed, memory pages are accounted for in the paging file and the process does not experience an address violation. Routine VirtualAlloc has the following calling sequence:

```
VirtualAlloc (
    LPVOID Address,      /* Pointer to virtual memory area */
    DWORD Size,          /* # bytes to reserve or commit */
    DWORD Type,          /* MEM_RESERVE and/or MEM_COMMIT */
    DWORD Prot);         /* Set for no access, read only or reading
                            and writing */
```

The Type argument can specify both reserving and committing in the same call. Routine VirtualFree is used to change a portion of committed memory to reserved memory or to release a portion of memory. VirtualFree has the following calling sequence:

```
VirtualFree (
    LPVOID Address, /* Base address of affected memory area */
    DWORD Size,     /* Amount of memory affected */
    DWORD Type);    /* MEM_DECOMMIT or MEM_RELEASE */
```

## Microsoft Windows — Sharing Memory

The Win32 API provides a means of sharing information stored in memory by mapping to a disk file. A file map is another object created in the Win32 environment that allows this capability. Memory used in this manner is automatically committed. The first step in using file mapping is to call CreateFile to actually create a file. CreateFile returns a file handle that is used in the next routine, CreateFileMapping:

```
MapObjectHandle = CreateFileMapping (
    HANDLE File,
    LPSECURITY_ATTRIBUTES SecAttrib,
    DWORD Protection,
    DWORD MaxSizeHigh,
    DWORD MaxSizeLow,
    LPSTR MapName);
```

Argument File is the handle of the file created from calling routine CreateFile. The security attributes argument describes a security structure pertinent to a Windows NT environment only. If no security concerns exist, NULL can be passed for this argument. Argument Protection can be set to allow reading and writing or just reading. Because files in the NTFS file system in Windows NT can be extraordinarily large, two double words, MaxSizeHigh and MaxSizeLow, are required to specify the amount of the file to be mapped. The last argument, MapName, is the name used to refer to this mapped file object. Calling CreateFileMapping only creates the mapped object; no memory address space has been associated with the mapping. This function is accomplished with a call to MapViewOfFile, as follows:

```
Address = MapViewOfFile (
        HANDLE MapObjectHandle,
        DWORD Access,
        DWORD OffsetHigh,
        DWORD OffsetLow,
        DWORD BytesMapped);
```

Argument MapObjectHandle represents the mapped object handle obtained by calling CreateFileMapping. Access indicates whether reading, writing, or both are allowed. The entire file is not necessarily mapped; the beginning byte of the file that is mapped is specified by arguments OffsetHigh and OffsetLow. The number of bytes mapped is specified by the final argument BytesMapped. Any process can now map to this memory by specifying the name of the mapped object in a call to routine OpenFileMapping as follows:

```
MapObjectHandle = OpenFileMapping (
        DWORD Access,
        BOOL Inherit,
        LPSTR MapName);
```

Argument `Access` has the same implications as it did in routine `MapViewOfFile`. `Inherit` is a boolean argument that controls whether a child process or thread could obtain the handle of this mapped object. The last argument, `MapName`, is the name of the mapped object being shared.

## Microsoft Windows — Pipes

The Win32 API provides for creating unnamed and named pipes. Unnamed pipes are created by calling routine `CreatePipe` as follows:

```
CreatePipe (
    PHANDLE ReadHandle,
    PHANDLE WriteHandle,
    LPSECURITY_ATTRIBUTES SecAttrib,
    DWORD Size);
```

Win32 unnamed pipes are unidirectional. The creating process must pass the read and write handles, `ReadHandle` and `WriteHandle`, to other processes that desire to use the pipe.

Named pipes are full-duplex. Other processes can affiliate with a named pipe by specifying its name through the `CreateFile` routine. A named pipe is created as follows:

```
Handle = CreateNamedPipe (
    LPTSTR PipeName,      /* Name of pipe */
    DWORD Access,         /* Controls information flow */
    DWORD Mode,           /* Byte or message mode */
    DWORD MaxInst,        /* How many copies of pipe */
    DWORD OutBufSize,     /* Max. buffer size outbound data */
    DWORD InBufSize,      /* Max. buffer size inbound data */
    DWORD Timeout,        /* Client connection wait time */
    LPSECURITY_ATTRIBUTES SecAttrib);
```

The `Access` argument controls information flow relative to the server. For example, setting this argument to `PIPE_ACCESS_OUTBOUND` allows the server to write and the client to read. The `Mode` argument determines the style of message transferred. Message mode means that messages are sent with a header. The header is transparent to the program and relieves the programmer from having to know the number of bytes to input. The `Mode` argument can also control whether the pipe is blocking or nonblocking. Nonblocking pipes do not wait for certain conditions such as a process performing a read from a pipe for which there is no data. MaxInst controls how many simultaneous connects to this pipe can exist. The buffer size arguments OutBufSize and InBufSize determine the largest amounts of data that can be input or output.

Clients connecting to named pipes use the CreateFile routine as follows:

```
Handle = CreateFile (
    LPCSTR PipeName,       /* Name of pipe */
    DWORD Access,          /* Controls information flow */
    DWORD ShareMode,       /* Set to zero */
    LPSECURITY_ATTRIBUTES SecAttrib,
    DWORD CreateFlag,      /* Set to OPEN_EXISTING */
    DWORD PipeFlag,        /* Set to FILE_FLAG_OVERLAPPED or
                              FILE_FLAG_WRITE_THROUGH */
    Handle Temp);          /* Ignored */
```

The ramifications of the PipeFlag argument are related to how the client controls network buffering and asynchronous I/O independent of the server.

## UNIX — Solaris and Linux Standard File I/O

The following file management routines are found in both Solaris and Linux:

```
open          unlink
stat          chmod
read          chown
write         mknod
lseek         close
link
```

The open routine is used to create or open a file for reading or writing and has the following arguments:

```
fd = open (
    char* filename,    /* File name */
    int mode,          /* File use orientation */
    int perm );        /* Access permissions */
```

Routine open returns a *file descriptor*, which is used in all subsequent file I/O calls related to this file. The read and write function calls are performed as follows:

```
stat = write (
    int fd,             /* File descriptor */
    char* buffer,       /* Output buffer */
    int count );        /* How many chars to output */

stat = read (
    int fd,             /* File descriptor */
    char* buffer,       /* Input buffer */
    int count );        /* How many chars to input */
```

Argument stat will contain the actual number of bytes transacted or a −1 if an error occurs. When the file is no longer required, the file descriptor is freed by calling routine close as follows:

```
stat = close (fd);
```

UNIX files are accessed as a series of bytes. I/O can be performed starting at any byte within a particular file. The byte starting position can be established by calling routine lseek as follows:

```
lseek (
    int fd,         /* File descriptor */
    long offset,    /* Starting byte position */
    int mode );     /* Relative starting position */
```

The last argument, mode, refers to whether the starting position is relative to the start of the file (I_SET), to the current position (I_CUR), or to the end of the file (I_END). Read and write operations take place at the new position established by the call to lseek.

Linking files in UNIX means creating another name for the file. Specifically, a call to routine link establishes a hard link and is called as follows:

```
link ( char *origname, char* newname );
```

A hard link is cancelled by calling routine unlink as follows:

```
unlink ( char* newname );
```

File ownership can be established by calling routine chown as follows:

```
chown (
    char* filename,
    int ownerid,
    int groupid );
```

The ownerid and groupid are established when a user account is set up on the system and could be obtained from your system administrator.

The permissions associated with a file can also be established by calling routine chmod as follows:

```
chmod (
    int fd,
    int mode );
```

Argument fd is the file descriptor of the file and mode represents the bit mask that reflects the new permissions setting. This mask is based on the sequence rwxrwxrwx where each group of rwx is the kind of access (read, write, execute) that is possible for the owner of the file, the file group, and the world. For example, a mode setting of 666 means all the entities have read and write access to the file.

Routine mknod is used to create special and regular files. Files can be directories, a named pipe, a character-oriented file, a block-oriented file, or a regular file. Our discussion of mknod focuses on named pipes. The calling sequence to mknod is as follows:

```
mknod ( char* filename, int type, int device );
```

The type argument indicates what kind of file is being created and can be set as follows:

| | |
|---|---|
| S_IFDIR | Directory |
| S_IFCHR | Character-oriented file |
| S_IFBLK | Block-oriented file |
| S_IFREG | Regular file |
| S_IFIFO | Names pipe |

The last argument, device, is pertinent only when you are creating character-oriented or block-oriented files.

# UNIX — Solaris Asynchronous File I/O

Asynchronous file operations can be performed in Solaris with the aio routines. The asynchronous file I/O operations require the establishment

of an asynchronous I/O control block structure that has the following
elements:

```
struct aiocb {
    int aio_fildes;             /* File descriptor */
    volatile void *aio_buf;     /* Data buffer */
    size_t aio_nbytes;          /* Transfer size */
    off_t aio_offset;           /* File offset */
    int aio_reqprio;            /* Request priority */
    struct sigevent aio_sigevent; /* signal # */
    int aio_lio_opcode;         /* listio operation */
};
struct sigevent {
    int sigev_notify;           /* notification mode */
    int sigev_signo;            /* signal number */
    union sigval sigev_value;   /* signal value */
};

union sigval {
    int sival_int;
    void *sival_ptr;
};
```

The `aio_offset` element specifies where in the file the I/O operation is to begin and must be specified for every `aio` request. The
signal information specified in the `aiocb` structure element
`aio_sigevent` is posted when the I/O operation completes. The
`aio_lio_opcode` and `aio_reqprio` are ignored by the `aio_read` and
`aio_write` routines. The asynchronous read and write operation
calls are performed as follows:

```
int aio_read(struct aiocb *aiocbptr);

int aio_write(struct aiocb *aiocbptr);
```

The status of an asynchronous I/O request can be obtained by calling
routine `aio_return` as follows:

```
ssize_t aio_return (struct aiocb *aiocbptr);
```

This routine will return the number of bytes read or written into element `aio_nbytes`. Routine `aio_error` is called to return any error status
generated by the specified `aio` operation and is called as follows:

```
int aio_error (const struct aiocb *aiocbptr);
```

Calling either `aio_return` or `aio_error` counts as a use of the `aiocb`
structure, invalidating it for further use until the appropriate values
such as `aio_offset` are initialized.

## Microsoft Windows — Standard UNIX File I/O

All of the file operations described for UNIX in the previous section are available in several of the Microsoft programming environments, such as Visual C/C++ or Borland C/C++.

## Microsoft Windows — Synchronous and Asynchronous File I/O

The Win32 API provides both synchronous and asynchronous API routines. The same routines are used in both cases, except that for asynchronous file I/O the definition of an *overlapped* structure is required:

```
struct _OVERLAPPED {
    DWORD SysStatus;          /* System status returned */
    DWORD AmtDataXfer;        /* Amount of data xferred */
    DWORD LowOffset;          /* Low order offset value */
    DWORD HighOffset;         /* High order offset value */
    HANDLE Event;             /* Event signaled when done */
    } OVERLAPPED;
```

The overlapped structure indicates where I/O is to take place in the place by specifying the appropriate offset in elements LowOffset and HighOffset. Two double words are required to accommodate the file position, because files in the NTFS file system found under Windows NT can be huge ($2^{64}$ bytes!). Element Event can specify an event object that can be signaled to indicate the completion of the I/O request. ReadFile and WriteFile are used to perform the I/O. The specification of NULL for the overlapped structure implies synchronous I/O. These routines have the following calling sequence:

```
ReadFile (
    HANDLE Handle,            /* File handle */
    LPVOID Buffer,            /* Buffer to hold input */
    DWORD InputBytes,         /* Number bytes to read */
    LPDWORD BytesRead,        /* Number bytes actually read */
    LPOVERLAPPED OverLap );   /* For asynchronous I/O */

WriteFile (
    HANDLE Handle,            /* File handle */
    LPVOID Buffer,            /* Buffer to hold output */
    DWORD OutputBytes,        /* Number bytes to output */
    LPDWORD BytesOutput,      /* Number bytes actually output */
    LPOVERLAPPED OverLap );   /* For asynchronous I/O */
```

The handle specified as an argument to these routines is obtained from a call to routine CreateFile, which has the following calling sequence:

```
Handle = CreateFile (
        LPCTSTR Filename,
        DWORD Access,
        DWORD ShareMode,
        LPSECURITY_ATTRIBUTES SecAttrib,
        DWORD CreateAction,
        DWORD FileAttrib,
        HANDLE HPFSKey );
```

The Access argument is set to indicate whether the file will be created for reading, writing, or both. The ShareMode argument indicates whether the file will be shared for reading, writing, or both. The security attributes argument specifies the security structure pertinent to NT environments only. The CreateAction argument specifies how to behave when the file is created and whether another copy of the file already exists.

## Microsoft Windows — Controlling File Access

File access can be explicitly controlled with the LockFile and UnlockFile routines. LockFile allows the caller to specify a certain area of a file that cannot be accessed either by reading or writing and has the following calling sequence:

```
LockFile (
        HANDLE File,
        DWORD LowOffset,
        DWORD HighOffset,
        DWORD LowBytestoLock,
        DWORD HiBytestoLock);
```

Notice the two double words required to accommodate the number of bytes of the file to lock. To undo the effect of LockFile routine, UnLockFile is called, which has the same calling arguments.

# Chapter 5

# Networking Facilities

Networking is an integrated part of both UNIX and the Microsoft Windows environments. This chapter will discuss networking configuration and facilities available in both environments including TCP/IP, remote procedure calls (RPCs), sockets, and network file services (NFS). This chapter assumes the reader has some familiarity with certain basic network terms and concepts. It answers the following questions:

- What networking protocols are supported?
- How are network devices installed and managed?
- What are remote procedure calls and how are they used?
- What are sockets and how are they used to perform networking operations?
- How can remote disks or file systems be mounted to appear locally?
- What kind of dial-up networking support exists?

## UNIX — Solaris Network Configuration Files and Databases

The files and databases listed in Table 5.1 are key to the successful configuration of a network.

| File/database | Purpose |
| --- | --- |
| /etc/hostname.interface | Contains the host name or IP address associated with the machine–network interface |
| /etc/nodename | Contains host name of local machine |
| /etc/defaultdomain | Contains the name of the administrative domain to which this machine belongs |
| /etc/defaultrouter | Will contain an entry for each router directly connected to the network |
| /etc/hosts | Contains IP addresses and host names of all machines on the network |
| /etc/inet/hosts | Host database for local name service |

**Table 5.1.** *Solaris network configuration files and databases*

## UNIX — Solaris — Networking with PPP

The PPP software may not be present on your system if a customized installation was performed. PPP must be installed on every machine involved with the network configuration. For configurations not using a name service, the names of all participating machines must be entered into the /etc/inet/hosts files on each node that is part of the network. This file will contain the IP address and its associated node name. PPP nodes are typically named with a -ppp suffix.

PPP under Solaris is integrated with the uucp facility. Several files that are part of the uucp database are involved:

| | |
| --- | --- |
| /etc/uucp/Devices | Contains an entry for every communications device host uses |
| /etc/uucp/Dialers | Contains entries describing modem commands for endpoint PPP communications |
| /etc/uucp/Systems | Contains entries for every machine to which local host can dial out |

The Solaris PPP software comprises the following components:

| | |
|---|---|
| `/usr/sbin/asppd` | The link manager, a user-level daemon that automates a PPP connection to a remote host |
| `/usr/sbin/aspppls` | Special PPP connection login shell |
| `/etc/asppp.cf` | Link manager configuration file that describes endpoint communications characteristics |
| `/var/adm/log/asppp.log` | PPP link manager report log |
| `/tmp/.asppp.fifo` | Pipe file used to facilitate communications between `aspppd` and `aspppls` |

PPP users are logged in under a special shell, `aspppls`. The following is a sample entry from the `passwd` file reflecting PPP user `merusi`.

```
....
merusi:jk29dls43:10:50:Don Merusi:/:/usr/sbin/asppls
....
```

The `/etc/shadow` file must also be updated for all the login names used by every PPP endpoint machine.

## UNIX — Solaris — Network Name Services

Solaris supports two name services, DNS (Domain Name Service) and NIS+ (Network Information Service). NIS+ is specific to the Solaris environment and performs a combination of DNS functionality along with distributed user account management. There is really no counterpart to NIS+ in the Microsoft Windows environment and we therefore focus our discussion on DNS. Solaris DNS clients rely on two files:

```
resolv.conf and /etc/nsswitch.conf
```

The `resolv.conf` file lists the addresses of the servers where network node names can be resolved. This file also provides the name of the local domain and the location of name servers. The following is a sample of the contents of the `resolv.conf` file:

```
domain merusi.org
; local name server
nameserver 127.0.0.1
; other name servers to try
nameserver 191.29.50.20
nameserver 191.29.60.30
```

The `nsswitch.conf` file is unique to Solaris and contains fifteen types of information and the associated sources of that information. Each source is investigated one line at a time until the requested information is found. Some lines contain more than one source. If the information search is unsuccessful at the first specification, the second one is used. Sources are netmasks, `passwd` files, aliases services, and many other items. The source specification can be one of the following:

| | |
|---|---|
| *file* | Local file stored in the client's `/etc` directory |
| *NIS* | An NIS map |
| *NIS+* | An NIS+ table |
| *DNS* | DNS for host names |

Search criteria can be defined that describes what action to take depending on the success of the information search. For example, in Figure 5.1, `[NOTFOUND=return]` means the source responded with *No such entry* and the action is to return. Notice that some of the lines contain more than one source, which means that an NIS map will be consulted first, and if the information is not found there, a local file will be consulted. Figure 5.1 is a sample of some entries in an `nsswitch.conf` file.

```
passwd:        files nis
group:         files nis
hosts:         nis [NOTFOUND=return]  files
networks:      nis [NOTFOUND=return]  files
protocols:     nis [NOTFOUND=return]  files
rpc:           nis [NOTFOUND=return]  files
ethers:        nis [NOTFOUND=return]  files
netmasks:      nis [NOTFOUND=return]  files
bootparams:    nis [NOTFOUND=return]  files
publickey:     nis [NOTFOUND=return]  files
netgroup:      nis
automount:     files nis
aliases:       files nis
```

**Figure 5.1.** *A sample* `nsswitch.conf` *file*

DNS servers require several more files in addition to the two previously mentioned. Boot and data files must be established as follows:

| | |
|---|---|
| `named.boot` | Establish server as primary, secondary, or caching-only |
| `named.ca` | Establish names of root server and addresses |
| `hosts` | All data about machines and local zone |
| `hosts.rev` | Specifies a zone in the IN-ADDR domain for reverse mapping |
| `named.local` | Specifies address for local loopback |

A complete discussion of setting up a DNS server is beyond the scope of this book.

## UNIX — Linux — Network Configuration Files and Databases for SLIP, PLIP, and PPP Connections

Two files are key to successful networking in the Slackware version of Linux:

```
/etc/hosts
/etc/networks
```

The `/etc/hosts` file fulfills the same purpose as the `/etc/inet/hosts` file, as described earlier for the Solaris environment, and is used to support a local network name service. The `/etc/networks` file is used to list the names of the various networks in which the system will take part. Using network names is also more convenient than attempting to remember IP addresses, and it makes establishing static routes easier. The `/etc/networks` files lists the network name with only the network part of the IP address.

An Ethernet communications interface is activated by using the `ifconfig` command as follows:

```
ifconfig interface [[-net] [-host] address [options]]
```

The `ifconfig` command assigns the IP address to the interface as follows:

```
ifconfig interface address
```

Several other options can also be specified with `ifconfig`, including the following (we assumed that readers have some familiarity with TCP/IP network addressing conventions):

| | |
|---|---|
| net | Treat address as a network address |
| host | Treat address as a host address |
| netmask addr | IP network mask for specified interface |
| metric N | Establish cost factor for routing through this interface |
| address | IP address assigned to this interface |

The ifconfig command can also be used to query a network interface as follows:

```
$ /sbin/ifconfig eth0
eth0      Link encap:10Mbps Ethernet  HWaddr 00:00:C0:CA:4C:18
          inet addr:191.29.73.52  Bcast:191.29.255.255
Mask:255.255.0.0
          UP BROADCAST RUNNING MULTICAST  MTU:1500  Metric:1
          RX packets:349080442 errors:1 dropped:41 overruns:0
          TX packets:195034 errors:13 dropped:0 overruns:0
          Interrupt:5 Base address:0x250 Memory:d0000-d2000
```

Parallel IP (PLIP) connections can be established with the ifconfig command by using the following command:

```
ifconfig plip0 unix1 pointopoint unix2
```

This command says to activate a parallel-IP device plip0 with the IP address of node unix1. The address at the other end of the line is resolved from the name unix2. SLIP (Serial line IP) and PPP (Point-to-Point) protocols are managed with other commands. The Dial-up Protocol Driver is a convenient utility for establishing SLIP connections in Linux and has the following format:

```
dip [-tvi] [scriptfile]
```

| | |
|---|---|
| -t | Run the dip utility in command mode, enter commands directly |
| -v | Use with -t to display error level |
| -i | Operate dip in input mode as SLIP server to other users, used with diplogin |
| scriptfile | File containing dip commands |

The following are a few dip commands that can be entered manually (-i) or by putting them into a script file:

| `dial num` | Dial specified phone number |
|---|---|
| `help` | Ask for help on a specific command |
| `modem type` | Indicate modem manufacturer (e.g., Hayes) |
| `speed num` | Specify line speed (baud rate) |
| `if $var of number` | Conditional if test (used with `goto` label) |
| `goto label` | Jump to label in `dip` script |

`dip` script files can contain conditional logic tests and branch commands. `dip` script files understand a set of predefined variables, some of which are the following:

| `$local` | Host name of local machine |
|---|---|
| `$locip` | IP address of local machine |
| `$rmtip` | IP address of remote machine |
| `$errlvl` | Result code of last command |

The `/etc/diphosts` file is used to control what users and what machines can make SLIP connections. The `diphosts` file contains a series of entries specifying the user ID, password, host name, or IP address of the calling machine and other connection parameters.

PPP connections are most conveniently managed by using the `pppd` daemon and `chat` programs. Typically, PPP networking is performed by logging into the remote host with some communications program and manually starting the `pppd` daemon there and on the local machine. A `chat` script can automate this procedure. The `chat` utility is invoked as follows:

```
chat [options] script
```

Some of the `chat` utility options are as follows:

| `-f filename` | File containing chat script commands |
|---|---|
| `-v` | Log `chat` output to `syslog` |
| `-t` | Specify time out between commands |

The `pppd` daemon must be activated as follows:

```
pppd [options] [tty_name] [speed]
```

There are more than forty `pppd` commands, and a comprehensive discussion of all of them is beyond the scope of this book. However, the following represents a basic `pppd` command:

```
pppd /dev/cua0 28800 connect 'chat -f myunix.chat'
```

This command says to connect at 28,800 baud through dial-up device `/dev/cua0` and use the commands in the chat script `myunix.chat`.

## UNIX — Establishing DNS with Linux

Configuring DNS (*Domain Name Service*) in Slackware Linux is similar to Solaris and involves several different files. The local resolver is configured in file `/etc/host.conf`. A resolver is a program that extracts DNS information from a name server. A name server is another machine that provides the mapping of domain names to IP addresses. Commands in the `/etc/host.conf` file can instruct the local resolver to do such tasks as check for IP spoofing, produce an alert if spoofing is attempted, or resolve network names through DNS first rather than resorting to a local host name table.

File `/etc/resolv.conf` is used to tell the local resolver how to use DNS to resolve names. Two pieces of information are generally stored in this file. The domain name is specified here to allow the resolver to perform a best guess about the name of a node we are trying to access. The primary name server is also specified in this file. The primary name server is the machine we use to resolve our host names if our best-guess attempts are unsuccessful.

The `named` daemon is the critical program that makes DNS work. This program is activated at boot time and uses a set of configuration files to establish its operating environment. `named` listens for DNS requests on a default network port specified in the `/etc/services` files.

## UNIX — Solaris and Linux — Mounting Remote Disks with NFS

The *Network File System* (NFS) is the premier mechanism that enables disks physically installed at a remote location to be mounted as if they were local. NFS operations are convenient for allowing diskless workstations to function as if they had hard drives installed. The ability to perform this operation is easily managed by specifying some extra information as part of the `mount` command, as follows:

```
# mount -t nfs -o intr,hard farnode:/bin/work /mnt
```

This command mounts the directory `/bin/work` located on node `farnode` to a local mount point named `/mnt`. All references to `/mnt` on the local node will appear like any other directory area. The `-t` option refers to the particular kind of file-system mount being performed. In this case, the file system type is NFS. The `-o` options of `hard` and `intr` mean that the mount request will persist until a connection is made to `farnode` and that file operations can be interrupted.

## Network Configuration under Microsoft Windows

All network configuration and management is performed either from the **Network** icon found on the **Control Panel** screen or from the **Dial-up Networking** icon found in the **My Computer** shortcut. If more than one dial-up configuration is going to be configured, the **Network** icon in the **Control Panel** is not used. The **Network** icon is more appropriate for systems connected directly on a network, such as through Ethernet to a LAN. However, settings can be made in this configuration window that are applied to all other network connections made by this system. Double-clicking on the **Dial-up Networking** icon produces another window displaying all of the dial-up configurations for this machine. Figure 5.2 illustrates the dial-up configurations present on the author's PC at home. Right-clicking on a particular dial-up configuration pops up a submenu listing various options. Choosing **Properties** creates another display indicating more specific information about the network connection, as illustrated in Figure 5.2.

The two buttons at the bottom of the display in Figure 5.3 allow more comprehensive configuration of the connection. The **Configure** button brings you to a window, illustrated in Figure 5.4, that lets you configure such characteristics as line speed, COM port, and FIFO buffering.

**Figure 5.2.** *Dial-up networks available on the author's home PC*

**Figure 5.3.** *The result of right-clicking on the TIAC shortcut from Figure 5.2 and then choosing Properties*

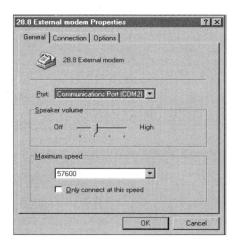

**Figure 5.4.** *Result of clicking on the* **Configure** *button from Figure 5.3*

The **Connection** tab brings up a window allowing the control of the number of data bits, the number of stop bits and the number of parity bits. The **Connection** tab window also lets you specify the action to be taken when a dial-up succeeds or fails. The **Options** tab window allows a special operator window to appear when a connection is made. The **Options** tab window also allows specification of whether modem status is to be displayed.

The **Server Type...** button produces the window shown in Figure 5.5. This window lets you specify the protocol to be used with this connection. Figure 5.5 indicates that the connection is a PPP (*Point-to-Point*) type. Other kinds of connections that can be configured here are NRN (*Netware Connect*) or Windows for Workgroups. Also, the TCP/IP network protocol will be used exclusively for all network communications. Depending on the network environment, the other protocols may be selected. More than one protocol can be selected simultaneously. The **TCP/IP Settings...** button brings you the window in Figure 5.6.

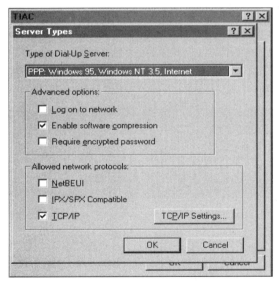

**Figure 5.5.** *The result of clicking on the* **Server Type...** *button from Figure 5.3*

The **TCP/IP Settings...** window allows the specification of the machine IP address, DNS address information, WINS address information, and routing information. Depending on the system being dialed up, the network address may be assigned by the server. If DNS or WINS is used, provision is made for a primary and secondary name server. In Figure 5.6, WINS is not used. For dial-up connections, routing specifics are generalized and the option of whether or not to use the default gateway on the remote node is the only choice. IP header compression can be used to streamline transmission time. Figure 5.7 illustrates the characteristics that can be set by clicking on the **Network** icon in the **Control Panel**. Configurations from this window are performed for each network adapter connected to your system. This feature is somewhat confusing with respect to dial-up adapters. Ordinarily, a network adapter makes a connection onto the network with a set of specific configuration definitions.

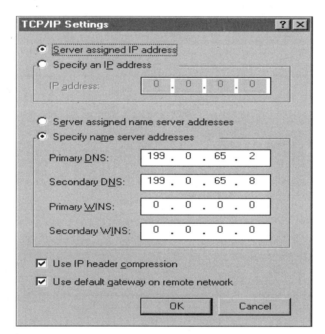

**Figure 5.6.** *TCP/IP settings window for TIAC dial-up network*

However, the dial-up adapter can connect to several different networks, and each connection requires its own specific configuration definitions. For example, dialing into an Internet service provider may require you to specify the IP address of the DNS primary server pertinent to your ISP's environment. However, when you dial into your company, the DNS information is different, and your system must be able to reference the appropriate information for a proper connection.

Notice in Figure 5.8 that more information about the nature of the network connection can be specified. A subnet mask can be specified along with the IP address in the IP tab window. In the **Gateway** tab window, a specific gateway machine can be specified. Clicking the other tabs lets you specify details about each network property.

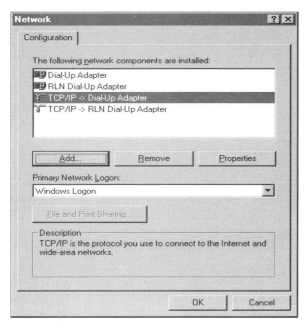

**Figure 5.7.** *A list of all network adapters installed on the author's PC; the window is the result of clicking on the* **Network** *shortcut from the* **Control Panel** *window*

## Microsoft Windows — Mounting Remote File Services

For security reasons, remote file services must be offered as shares before they can be accessed from a remote system. A share can be established for public access or to allow very specific access. The security system within Windows NT is very comprehensive and allows a wide range of access control to be established for particular share.

Mapping a disk drive is performed through the Explore utility. In Figure 5.9, the Explore utility is used to map a network drive by invoking the **Tools** pull-down menu and selecting **Map Network Drive...**, which results in Figure 5.10.

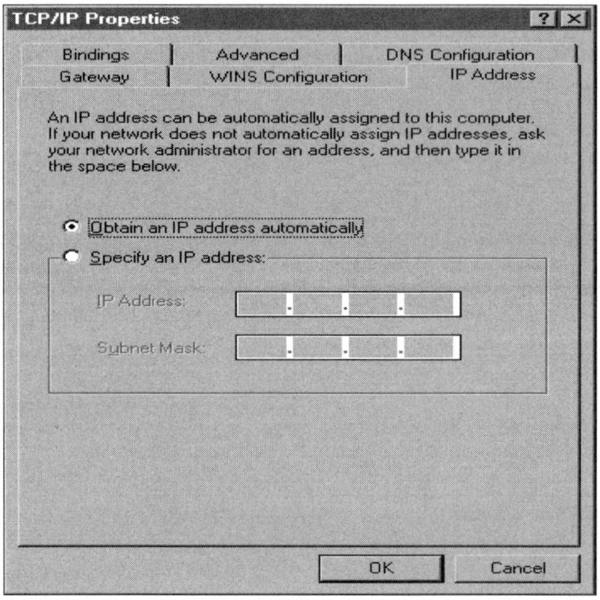

**Figure 5.8.** *Result of double-clicking on TCP/IP adapter*

**Figure 5.9.** *Mapping a network drive to a remote share*

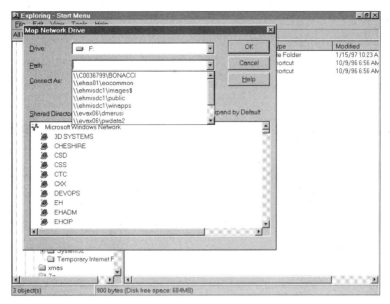

**Figure 5.10.** *Selecting a specific path to map to drive* `F`:

# Microsoft Windows — Remote Procedure Calls

Using RPCs in the world of Microsoft Windows is overwhelming. A comprehensive discussion about how to write an RPC application is beyond the scope of this book. The RPC mechanism incorporated by Microsoft originates from the Open Software Foundation and is the standard for the UNIX *Distributed Computing Environment* (DCE). When you write RPC applications, you must consider both the server and client side. Furthermore, the server and the client can be hetero- geneous — a Microsoft Windows client could be communicating with a Sun Workstation. The RPC mechanism functions in both the Windows NT and Windows 95 environments. A few exceptions exist in the Windows 95 environment — for example, named pipes are not supported as a protocol. A simple RPC application comprises the fol- lowing files:

- The function code
- An Interface Definition File
- An Attribute Control File
- The server body code
- The client body code

These files are incorporated together through a `makefile`. The function code represents the routine that will be called "over the network." The function code may be a sort routine, something that averages an array of numbers, or just about anything else. The *Interface Definition File* (IDL) is created by running the `uuidgen` utility (`uuidgen -i`). RPC applications require a unique identification for successful operation in a network. A *unique universal identifier* (`uuid`) is created that uniquely identifies the RPC server on the network. A `uuid` is a long string of numbers and letters contrived from the current time and machine ID. The IDL compiler, MIDL, uses information stored in the *Attribute Control File* (ACF) to determine whether automatic or manual bindings should be performed. Automatic binding means that the code will query the RPC name server and bind the client to the server. The basic server code call sequence is as follows:

```
    ...
/* Get all protocol and endpoint information generated
   in the IDL file */
RpcServerUseAllProtSeqsIf(...)
    ...
/* Let the server know about what interfaces can be
   called by the clients */
RpcServerRegisterIf(...)
    ...
/* Obtain list of all bindings provided by this server */
RpcServerInqBindings(...)
    ...
/* Tell RPC name server about this server so it can be
   publicized */
RpcNsBindingExport(...)
    ...
/* Listen for connection requests from clients */
RpcServerListen(...)
    ...
```

The client code is very simple, consisting essentially of the call to the RPC function. The client is actually indistinguishable as an RPC program except for certain header files (`.h`) required to build the program properly for the RPC environment.

## Microsoft Windows — Using Sockets (TCP and UDP Connections)

The concept of the socket originated in the Berkeley version of UNIX. A socket represents a full-duplex communication device. Sockets are usually bound or connected to ports. A port is merely a positive integer value. When a socket is bound to a port on a local machine, the port number is unique. Other machines on the network can bind with that port using the unique port number. Socket connections can be connect-oriented (TCP, point-to-point) or connectionless (UDP, mailslot). TCP socket communication can be routed, whereas UDP socket communication only works within the realm of a single network segment. UDP communications is unreliable and is generally not used. Our discussion focuses on TCP communications. The basic code fragments for a TCP receiver follow:

```
    ...
SOCKADDR_IN ServerSockAddr;
SOCKADDR_IN ClientSockAddr;
SOCKET ServerSckt;
SOCKET ClientSckt;
    ...
/* Initialize Windows socket DLL */
WSAStartup(...)
    ...
/* Establish information in socket structure, for port #, net-
work family (the internet) and network address */
ServerSockAddr.sin_port=htons(PORT);
ServerSockAddr.sin_family=AF_INET;
ServerSockAddr.sin_addr.s_addr=htons(INADDR_ANY);
    ...
/* Create a socket */
ServerSckt=socket(AF_INET,SOCK_STREAM,0);
    ...
/* Associate socket with network address */
bind(ServerSckt ... );
    ...
/* Let socket accept connections */
listen(ServerSckt ... );
    ...
/* Accept connection when received */
accept(ServerSckt ... );
    ...
/* Receive date */
recv( ... );
    ...
```

# Remote Procedure Calls in Solaris

The Solaris environment provides different levels of calling routines for RPC services. These levels provide various degrees of control based on the amount of information and code provided. The interface levels are *simplified*, *top level*, *intermediate level*, *expert level*, and *bottom level*. Each level provides a greater degree of control; however, more information must be specified to perform the RPC procedure. The following list shows what routines must be used at those levels to perform the indicated procedures.

## Simplified

| | |
|---|---|
| `rpc_reg` | Register RPC procedure |
| `rpc_call` | Call remote procedure |
| `rpc_broadcast` | Send call message to all transports |

## Top Level

| | |
|---|---|
| `clnt_create` | Indicate server location and transport |
| `svc_create` | Specify dispatch function |

## Intermediate Level

| | |
|---|---|
| `clnt_tp_create` | Create client handle for transport |
| `svc_tp_create` | Create server handle for transport |

## Expert Level

| | |
|---|---|
| `clnt_tli_create` | Create client handle for transport |
| `svc_tli_create` | Create server handle for transport |
| `rpcb_set` | Map RPC server to network address |
| `rpcb_unset` | Delete previous mapping |
| `svc_reg` | Associate program and version number with dispatch routine |
| `svc_unreg` | Delete previous association |

## Bottom Level

| | |
|---|---|
| `clnt_dg_create` | Create client handle for remote program using connectionless transport |
| `svc_dg_create` | Create server handle using connectionless transport |
| `clnt_vc_create` | Create client handle for remote program using connection-oriented transport |
| `svc_vc_create` | Create server handle using connection-oriented transport |

A comprehensive discussion of all of these routines is beyond the scope of this book. It is best to observe the basic framework involved using the simplified interface. The following program calls a hypothetical RPC program named MERUSIRPC and utilizes a type of service routine commonly used with RPC programs called *translation data routines* (XDRs). These routines are used to translate data between RPC calls made in a heterogeneous environment. For example, data being transferred between a Sun SPARC workstation and an Intel Pentium must be translated between big- and little-endian for proper data representation. This task is accomplished with the XDR routines. The following program fragment is incomplete and serves only as a basis for writing a more elaborate application.

```
#include <rpc/rpc.h>
#include <rpcsvc/merusirpc.h>
#include <stdio.h>
#include <utmp.h>

main(argc,argv)
    int argc;
    char **argv;
{
    ....
if(stat = rpc_call(
        argv[1],    Remote server name
        MERUSIRPC,      RPC program being called
        MERUSIVERS,     RPC program version
        MERUSINUM,      RPC program number
        xdrencode,      XDR encode routine
        xdrparam1,      XDR encode parameter
        xdrdecode,      XDR decode routine
        xdrparam2,      XDR decode parameter
        "visible");     Transport specification
    ....
Assume an answer returned here
    ....
exit(0);
}
```

If there are no XDR encode or decode parameters, xdr_void is specified for those calling arguments. The "visible" argument refers to rpc_call attempting to use all visible transports listed in the /etc/netconfig file. If the rpc_call does not return in a certain amount of time, an error status is returned. Controlling retry attempts must be performed with a lower-level form of RPC call.

# Chapter 6

## System Administration — User Management and Security

U NIX and Windows both provide a variety of system management facilities. Windows NT and UNIX contain many utilities for maintaining user accounts and system security. Windows 95 does not have the comprehensive system administration and security features contained in Windows NT.

- What files are critical to system operation?
- What is the registry and how does it control the system?
- How are users administered on the system?
- How is user access controlled?
- What are groups?
- How are privileges assigned to users?
- How are messages displayed to all system users?
- How are system events logged?
- How are printers managed?

## Microsoft Windows NT

Microsoft Windows 95 only requires a user to log in if the machine is part of a network. In Microsoft Windows NT, both server and workstation always require a user to log in, regardless of whether the machine is on a network. Networks can be configured in two different ways: as a *work group* or in a *domain*. We focus on the domain environment in this book, because that is how most PC LAN installations are configured. In a domain, client machines access a server machine to perform user account validation. You can determine to which domain your machine belongs by clicking **Settings** from the **Start** button and then clicking on the **Networks** icon. The display in Figure 6.1 appears.

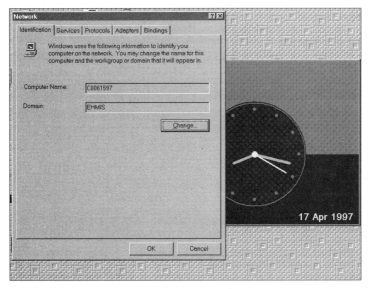

**Figure 6.1.** *The result of clicking on the network icon in the Control Panel; note the domain name*

Users are maintained by the **User Manager**. The initial screen for the **User Manager** utility appears in Figure 6.2. The **User Manager** displays what users and what types of users are valid on this machine.

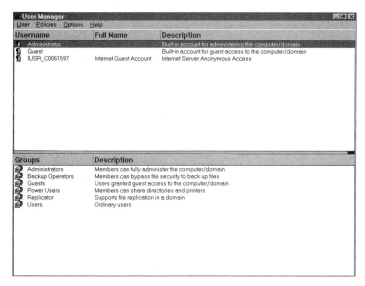

**Figure 6.2.** *The initial display for the User Manager*

Because the machine depicted is a client and is validated by another server, the list of authorized users on this machine is small. However, for demonstration purposes, new users could be added to be authorized locally by clicking on Users and then clicking on New Users. Figure 6.3 illustrates the resulting window.

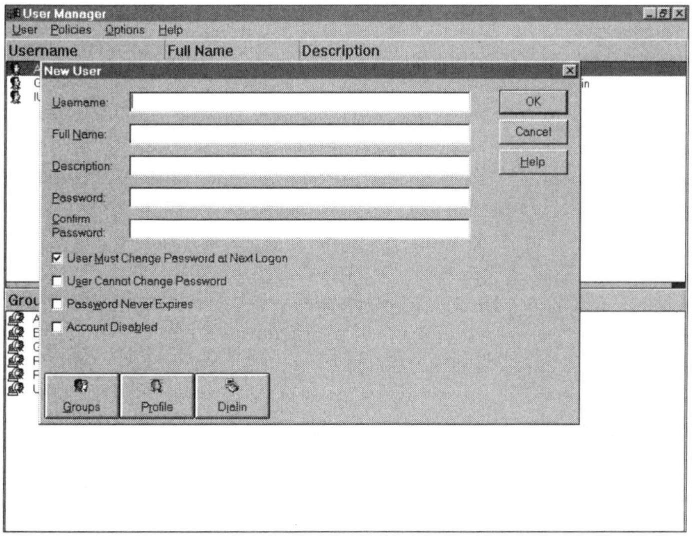

**Figure 6.3.** *Adding a new user*

Fields are presented for the user's login name, full name, description, and password. Other options allow control of password management. The three buttons at the bottom determine more characteristics of the user, including the group (**Group**) to which he or she belongs; information about the user (**Profile**), such as where his or her login script and home directory exist; and what kind of dial-in (**Dialin**) capability the user has. Figure 6.4 illustrates the result of clicking on the **Group** button.

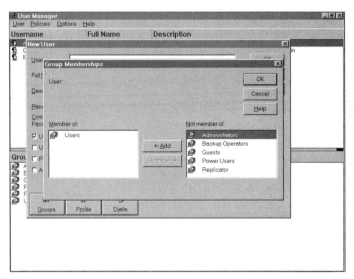

**Figure 6.4.** *Result of clicking on the Group button*

The new user is automatically assigned to group Users. Groups are a convenient means of assigning specific capability to a collection of users, rather than attempting to deal with a multitude of people individually. An individual's personal ID and group ID can have very different capability. The scroll window on the right in Figure 6.4 depicts other potential groups to which this user can be assigned. Certain groups are already established as part of the system environment:

| Group | Members can ... |
|---|---|
| *Administrators* | Completely administer computer/domain |
| *Backup operators* | Bypass security to back up files |
| *Guests* | Use system as a guest (generally read-only) |
| *Power users* | Share printers and directories |
| *Replicator* | Support file replication within domain |
| *Users* | Ordinary user |

New groups can be added by clicking on **User** and **New Local Group** in the **User Manager** main page. Figure 6.5 illustrates the resulting window.

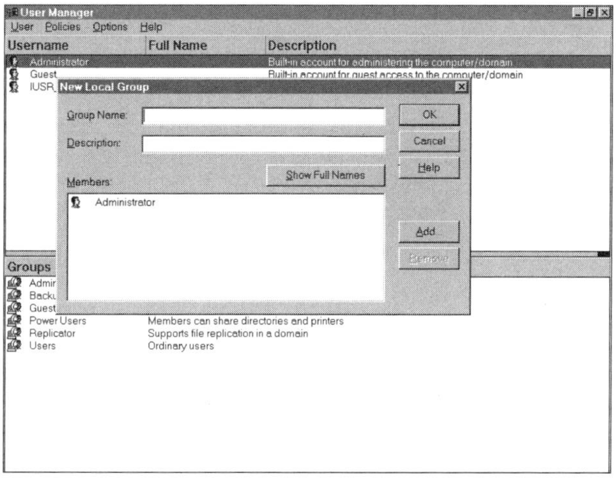

**Figure 6.5.** *Creating a new user group*

Highlighting an account name in the **User Manager** and clicking on **Policies** and then **Accounts** brings up the window in Figure 6.6. Account policy characteristics control mainly password management, such as when the password expires, maximum length, and whether or not to keep a password history.

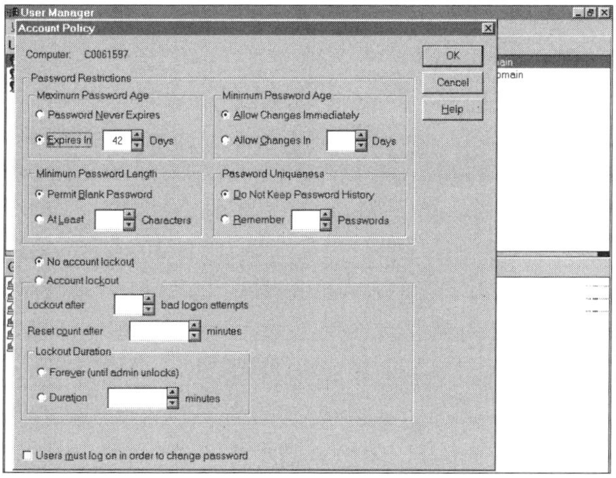

**Figure 6.6.** *Account policy characteristics*

On the same submenu, with a user account name highlighted, clicking on **User Rights Policy** produces the window in Figure 6.7.

The **User Rights Policy** screen lets you control user privilege, that is, what kinds of actions are legal for this user. The scroll window listing all potential privileges is created by clicking on the down arrow on the right-hand side of the **Rights** window. Controlling the kinds of actions described in this list is important because misuse of these functions can compromise the entire system.

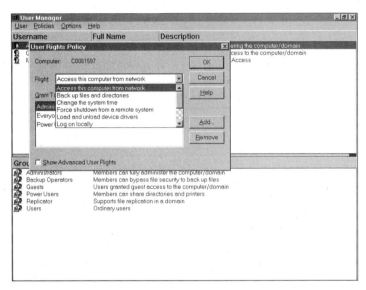

**Figure 6.7.** *The User Rights Policy window*

To provide an even more secure environment, various user activities can be audited for a particular account. Highlighting an account in the **User Manager** screen, clicking on **Policies**, then **Audit...** produces the screen shown in Figure 6.8. Auditing is either on or off for a particular user. If auditing is turned on, up to eight different activities can be monitored when this account:

- Logs on or off
- Performs file or object access
- Takes advantage of its personal rights
- Takes advantage of its group rights
- Performs any security policy changes
- Performs any system restart and shutdown
- Performs process tracking

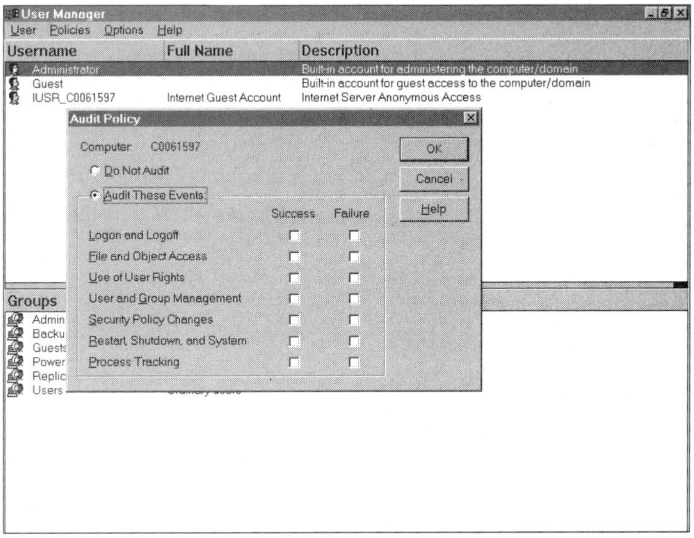

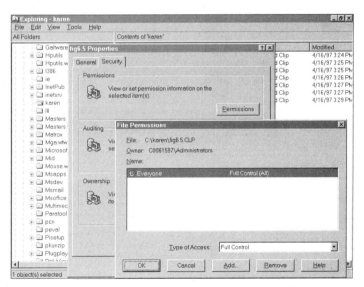

**Figure 6.8.** *The user account audit screen for administrator*

User account administration is especially pertinent with regard to accessing disk files. To determine what kind of protection exists for a particular disk file, you can right-click on the name of the file in the Explorer utility, then choose Permissions. Figure 6.9 illustrates the results of performing this function.

**Figure 6.9.** *Window resulting from clicking the right-hand mouse button over a file name in the Explorer utility and then choosing Permissions*

All protection functions for the file can be selected by clicking on the **Security** tab. File permissions, auditing, and ownership can be controlled from this window. When you click on the arrow on the right-hand side of the **Type of Access** window, you are presented with a list of access types. The type of access that is currently in effect for this file is displayed in the large window. For the file selected in Figure 6.9, **Everyone** has access and they can do every operation to this file. The **Add...** and **Remove** buttons let you grant and revoke permission for users or groups to access this file.

## Managing Printers in Microsoft Windows

Printer management under Microsoft Windows 95 and NT is performed with the Printer Manager. The Printer Manager facilitates installing, removing, and configuring printers both locally and on the network. The Printer Manager is invoked by clicking on the **Start** button, then clicking on **Settings**, and finally clicking on **Printers**, which results in a display showing all printers currently installed on your system, as depicted in Figure 6.10.

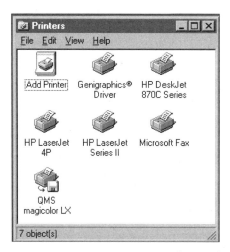

**Figure 6.10.** *Printers currently installed on the author's PC*

The dialog to add a printer is somewhat different in Windows NT and 95, but the overall procedure is similar. The Printer Installation

Wizard is activated by clicking on the Add Printer icon and eventually leads you to the screen illustrated in Figure 6.11. At this point you may choose a printer of which the Microsoft Windows environment is aware, or you may have to provide a disk from the printer manufacturer from which Windows will proceed to load the driver files.

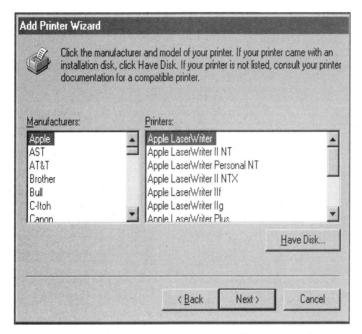

**Figure 6.11.** *The Printer Manager Installation Wizard screen*

## UNIX — Solaris and Linux User Administration

The /etc/passwd file is the focal point for user account administration in both Solaris and Linux UNIX. This is an ASCII text file that can be modified with your favorite editor, although that is not recommended. Typically, the vipw command is used to perform the editing function with whatever editor is defined with the EDITOR environment variable. The vipw command performs consistency checks on the password file and can only be activated by user root. Figure 6.12 is an example of the content of /etc/passwd.

```
root:gaevvP8dY47fE:0:1:system PRIVILEGED account:/:/bin/csh
nobody:*Nologin:65534:65534:anonymous NFS user:/:
nobodyV:*Nologin:60001:60001:anonymous SystemV.4 NFS user:/:
daemon:*:1:1:system background account:/:
bin:*:3:4:system librarian account:/bin:
uucp:Nologin:4:2:UNIX-to-UNIX
Copy:/usr/spool/uucppublic:/usr/lib/uucp/uucico
uucpa:Nologin:4:2:uucp administrative account:/usr/lib/uucp:
auth:*:6:11:Authentication Subsystem:/tcb/bin:
cron:*:7:14:Cron Subsystem:/usr/adm/cron:
lp:*:8:12:Line Printer Subsystem:/users/lp:
tcb:*:9:18:Trusted Computing Base:/tcb:
adm:*:10:19:Administration Subsystem:/usr/adm:
wnn:Nologin:12:1:Wnn System Account:/tmp:/bin/sh
+jas0055:::15:Jack Smith:/usr/users/jas0055:/bin/csh
+dem0023:::15:Don Merusi:/usr/users/dem0023:/bin/csh
+:*:
```

**Figure 6.12.** *Typical contents of* /etc/passwd *file*

Each line of the /etc/passwd file consists of seven fields:

- The login user name
- The encrypted password
- The UID (user ID) of the user
- The GID (group ID) of the user
- An identification field
- The home directory of this user
- The default shell for this user

Taking the last line in the password file, the login user name is merusi, the encrypted password follows, the UID is 11, the GID is 15, the descriptive field contains the user's name, the home directory is /usr/users/merusi, and the default shell is the C-shell. The implications of the UID and GID are apparent when dealing with file permissions. A disk file is associated with three types of access:

```
$ ls -l README
  -rw-r--r--  1 c081594 system  2563 Aug 1  14:45  README
```

The series -rw-r--r-- in the beginning of this long directory listing indicates what kind of access the file owner (rw-), the associated group(r-), and the world  (r--) have to this file. The file owner is c081594, and the group associated with this file is system. According to the permissions specification, the file owner can read and write this file, but could not execute it if it were a runnable program (no x in rw-). Anybody associated with group `system` can only read from this file. The world can only read from this file. The contents of the `/etc/group` file are illustrated in Figure 6.13.

```
system:*:0:root,merusi,smith
daemon:*:1:daemon
uucp:*:2:uucp
mem:*:3:
kmem:*:3:root
bin:*:4:bin,adm
sec:*:5:
mail:*:6:mail
terminal:*:7:
tty:*:7:root
news:*:8:uucp
opr:*:9:root
auth:*:11:
lp:*:12:
lpr:*:12:root
backup:*:13:
cron:*:14:
users:*:15:
sysadmin:*:16:
adm:*:19:adm
operator:*:20:
ris:*:21:
+:
```

**Figure 6.13.** *Contents of the* `/etc/group` *file*

Each line of the `/etc/group` file consists of four fields delimited by colons (`:`). The group is an ASCII text file and can be edited with your favorite editor. The first field represents the name of the group; the next field stands for whether a password is solicited or not. If this field is blank, no password is solicited. The next field contains the GID, and the last field consists of one or more user names that belong to the group. For example, in Figure 6.13 the first line of the `/etc/group` file is interpreted as follows: `system` is the group, the asterisk (`*`) implies that a password is required, the GID is 0, and the user IDs affiliated with this group are `root`, `merusi` and `smith`.

## The Solaris Admintool

The Solaris environment contains a GUI-oriented utility that can be used to manage users, groups, software products, printers, serial ports, and network hosts. This utility is `admintool` and is depicted in

Figure 6.14. The `admintool` utility allows you to manage six different system areas by clicking on the **Browse** pull-down menu and clicking on one of the choices. The admintool utility defaults to displaying information about users. When you click on one of the items from the Browse pull-down menu, another pull-down menu appears, presenting still more choices. If **Users** is selected, the choice of **Add** is available, and clicking on this item produces the display shown in Figure 6.15.

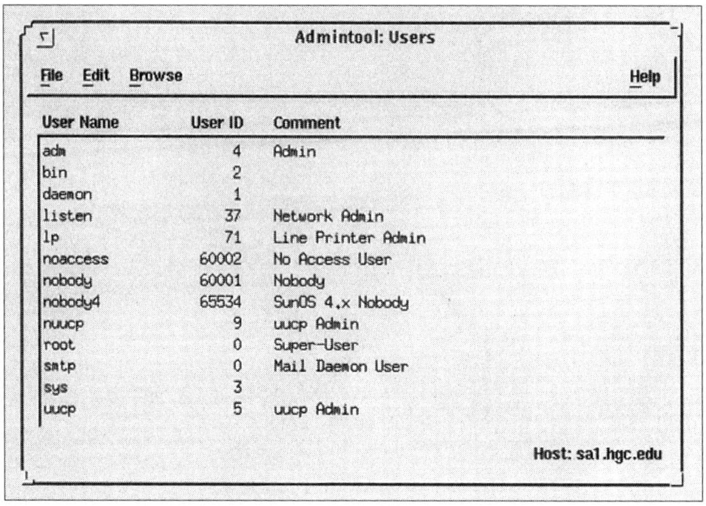

**Figure 6.14.** *Initial screen from Solaris Admintool*

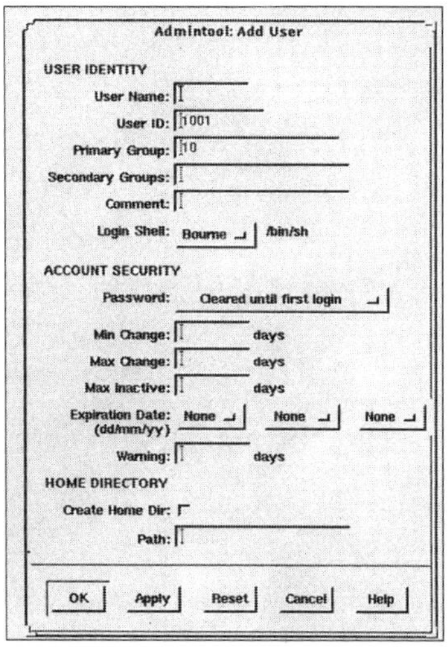

**Figure 6.15.** *Adding a user with the* `admintool` *utility*

The `admintool` utility can also be used to define printers on the system. The `admintool` utility allows you to specify the name of the printer and where it is served, as well as a short description of the printer such as its location. Figure 6.16 illustrates the `admintool` screen that lists printer information.

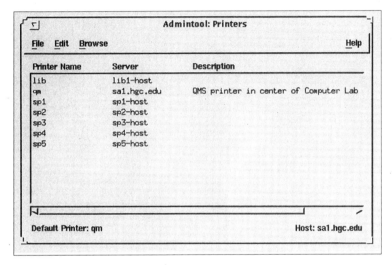

**Figure 6.16.** *The* `admintool` *printer management screen*

# Chapter 7

# Performance Monitoring

UNIX and Windows both provide facilities to monitor their environments to identify performance bottlenecks. Some of these performance utilities are system-wide, while others are process-specific. This chapter answers the following questions:

- What system-monitoring tools exist?
- What system-wide performance metrics can be tracked?
- What process-specific performance-measuring mechanisms exist?

## Solaris and Linix Performance Monitor — `perfmeter`

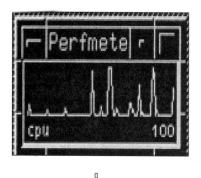

a                                                                b

**Figure 7.1.** *Sample* `perfmeter` *metric display for % CPU utilization: (a) strip chart style, (b) meter style*

The `perfmeter` utility is an OpenWindows-based visual performance monitor available in Solaris and Linux that displays the following information about the system environment:

- % CPU utilization
- Paging activity in pages/second
- Ethernet packets/second
- Number context switches/second
- Ethernet collisions/second
- Jobs swapped/second
- Disk transfers/second
- Number of device interrupts/second
- Number of errors/second on receiving packets
- Average number runnable processes over last minute

The `perfmeter` utility can be run in a variety of display configurations. Performance metrics can be displayed in the form of a strip chart or a dial meter. The meter contains an hour hand and a minute hand. The hour hand represents the metric average over a 20-second interval. The minute represents the metric average over 2 seconds. These displays are real-time and are adjusted according to run options. A single metric or all ten metrics can be displayed vertically or horizontally. The default display update rate is every 2 seconds. Figure 7.1 illustrates the % CPU utilization metric in both the strip-chart and meter styles.

perfmeter can display performance metrics for any node in the network. The only requirement for this to work is that the rstatd daemon be running on the system for which performance is being measured. perfmeter can accept a large variety of options:

| | |
|---|---|
| -a | Display all performance metrics concurrently |
| -g | Start display using strip charts |
| -d | Start display using meter dials |
| -l | Log performance samples to a file |
| -v | Show version number |
| -H | Display multiple metrics horizontally |
| -V | Display multiple metrics vertically |
| -s time | Specify sample time |
| q | Quit perfmeter |

All ten perfmeter metrics are illustrated in a horizontal orientation in Figure 7.2.

**Figure 7.2.** *Sample* perfmeter *display with all metrics displayed as meter dials*

Several varieties of perfmeter equivalents are available for Linux. The Internet is a vast source for this software, especially Sunsite.unc.edu/pub/Linux.

# UNIX — vmstat **in Solaris and Linux**

The vmstat command is another facility that can be used to determine system performance. vmstat has a small number of options but produces a very comprehensive report. On Solaris, the vmstat command is used as follows:

```
vmstat [ -cisS ] [ disks ] [interval] [ count] ]
```

-c    Cache flushing stats

-i    Display number interrupts/device

-s    Display total number of system events since boot time

-S    Report on swapping rather than paging activity

Disk names can be specified for the disks option. These disks are given priority by vmstat in its display. vmstat can also be run to display performance statistics every interval [count] seconds. Figure 7.3 illustrates the output from vmstat run with an interval specification. Each line is displayed every 3 seconds.

| procs | | | memory | | page | | | | | | | | disk | | | | faults | | | cpu | | | |
|---|---|---|---|---|---|---|---|---|---|---|---|---|---|---|---|---|---|---|---|---|---|---|---|
| r | b | w | swap | free | re | mf | pi | po | fr | de | sr | f0 | s3 | -- | -- | in | sy | cs | us | sy | id |
| 0 | 0 | 0 | 85064 | 11504 | 0 | 16 | 0 | 0 | 0 | 0 | 0 | 0 | 0 | 0 | 0 | 33 | 211 | 54 | 2 | 5 | 94 |
| 0 | 0 | 0 | 80884 | 9632 | 0 | 7 | 0 | 0 | 0 | 0 | 0 | 0 | 0 | 0 | 0 | 2 | 5 | 15 | 0 | 0 | 99 |
| 0 | 0 | 0 | 81100 | 9704 | 0 | 1 | 0 | 0 | 0 | 0 | 0 | 0 | 0 | 0 | 0 | 6 | 16 | 19 | 0 | 1 | 99 |
| 0 | 0 | 0 | 81540 | 9856 | 0 | 0 | 0 | 0 | 0 | 0 | 0 | 0 | 0 | 0 | 0 | 1 | 4 | 12 | 0 | 0 | 100 |
| 0 | 0 | 0 | 81540 | 9856 | 0 | 28 | 0 | 0 | 0 | 0 | 0 | 0 | 0 | 0 | 0 | 55 | 61 | 77 | 1 | 6 | 93 |
| 0 | 0 | 0 | 81540 | 9856 | 0 | 0 | 0 | 0 | 0 | 0 | 0 | 0 | 0 | 0 | 0 | 4 | 7 | 19 | 0 | 0 | 100 |
| 0 | 0 | 0 | 81540 | 9856 | 0 | 0 | 0 | 0 | 0 | 0 | 0 | 0 | 0 | 0 | 0 | 4 | 4 | 16 | 0 | 0 | 100 |
| 0 | 0 | 0 | 81532 | 9848 | 0 | 0 | 0 | 0 | 0 | 0 | 0 | 0 | 0 | 0 | 0 | 19 | 29 | 35 | 1 | 1 | 98 |
| 0 | 0 | 0 | 81520 | 9828 | 0 | 137 | 10 | 0 | 0 | 0 | 0 | 0 | 0 | 0 | 0 | 164 | 253 | 217 | 5 | 14 | 82 |
| 0 | 0 | 0 | 81172 | 9540 | 0 | 53 | 2 | 0 | 0 | 0 | 0 | 0 | 0 | 0 | 0 | 85 | 177 | 109 | 2 | 8 | 90 |
| 0 | 0 | 0 | 81152 | 9520 | 0 | 0 | 0 | 0 | 0 | 0 | 0 | 0 | 0 | 0 | 0 | 8 | 20 | 14 | 1 | 0 | 99 |

**Figure 7.3.** *The result of a* vmstat 3 *command*

The fields of vmstat in Solaris are interpreted as follows:

procs    # of processes in each state:

r    # processes waiting for CPU

b    # processes blocked

w    # processes runnable but swapped

memory    Real and virtual memory utilization

swap    Swap space available in KB

free    Free memory in KB

page      Paging activity (units per second)

   re      Pages reclaimed or swap-ins (-S)

   mf      Minor fault or swap-outs (-S)

   pi      KB paged in

   po      KB paged out

   fr      KB freed

   de      Short-term memory shortfall in KB

   sr      Pages scanned by clock algorithm

disk      Disk operations per second; up to four disks can be specified

faults      Trap/interrupt rates per second

   in      Non-clock-related device interrupts

   sy      System calls

   cs      CPU context switches

cpu      CPU utilization in percentage

   us      User time

   sy      System time

   id      Idle time

You must understand the nature of the operating-system environment to appreciate the meaning of `vmstat` information. For example, familiarity with the paging memory management environment of UNIX is important for properly interpreting the page activity field. The clock algorithm refers to the style by which the operating system reviews memory page status. All pages of memory are considered as if arranged about the dial of a clock. A conceptual software clock hand "ticks" by each page, evaluating what to do with it. This process usually continues until a certain predefined available memory threshold is attained.

The `vmstat` utility in the Slackware version of Linux is similar and has different options:

```
vmstat [-n] [delay] [count] [-V]
   -n            Display header only once
   delay         How many seconds between updates
   count         Number of updates produced; not specified = infinite
   -V            Display version number
```

Figure 7.4 illustrates the output from a vmstat command run under Linux. The output is more abbreviated than for Solaris.

```
procs                memory   swap      io    system        cpu
r b w  swpd  free  buff  si  so   bi   bo    in  cs  us sy id
0 0 0  1280  1012   856   0   0    3    0     2   4   0  0  0
0 0 0  1280  1012   856   0   0    0    0   192   7   1  2 97
0 0 0  1280  1012   856   0   0    0    0   163   6   1  2 96
0 0 0  1280  1012   856   0   0    0    0   146   4   1  3 96
0 0 0  1280  1012   856   0   0    0    2   147   4   1  2 97
0 0 0  1280  1012   856   0   0    0    0   169   7   1  3 96
0 0 0  1280  1012   856   0   0    0    0   167   5   2  3 95
0 0 0  1280  1012   856   0   0    0    0   157   4   1  2 97
0 0 0  1280  1012   856   0   0    0    0   142   4   1  3 96
0 0 0  1280  1012   856   0   0    0    1   147   4   2  2 96
0 0 0  1280  1012   856   0   0    0    0   170   8   0  3 96
0 0 0  1280  1012   856   0   0    0    0   157   6   2  2 96
```

**Figure 7.4.** *Output from a* vmstat 2 *command run under Linux*

The display is somewhat different from that under Solaris. There are no specific columns for disk activity. Also, there is less information about the paging environment.

```
Procs
   r          # processes waiting to run
   b          # processes in uninterruptible sleep
   w          # processes swapped out but runnable

Memory (KB)
   swpd       Amount of virtual memory used
   free       Amount of free memory
   buff       Amount of memory used as buffers

Swap
   si         Amount of memory swapped in from disk (KB/s)
   so         Amount of memory swapped out to disk (KB/s)
   bi         Blocks sent to a block device (Blocks/s)
   bo         Blocks received from a block device (Blocks/s)
```

```
System
    in              # interrupts per second
    cs              # context switches per second

CPU
    us              % of total CPU for user time
    sy              % of total CPU time for system time
    id              % of total idle CPU time
```

## Microsoft Windows

Windows NT has a Performance Monitor that provides a wealth of data about many aspects of the system, including processor, memory, and disk utilization. The performance information is displayed in a wraparound style in real time. The performance data can also be saved to a log file and subsequently played back. A limited reporting facility is available. Figure 7.5 illustrates how the Performance Monitor is invoked.

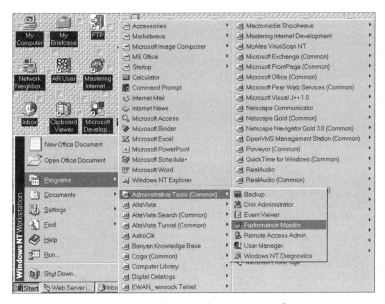

**Figure 7.5.** *Invoking the Windows NT Performance Monitor from the Administrative Tools menu*

After you select the Performance Monitor, the blank chart displayed in Figure 7.6 appears. You must select what metrics to display to observe performance data.

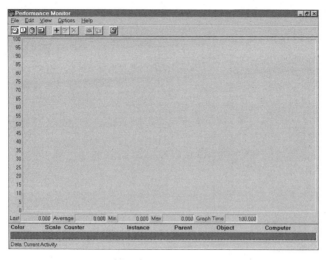

**Figure 7.6.** *Initial Performance Monitor display*

Clicking on the +-sign on the top toolbar presents you with a scrolling window listing all of the metrics available. In Figure 7.7, Processor metrics are displayed.

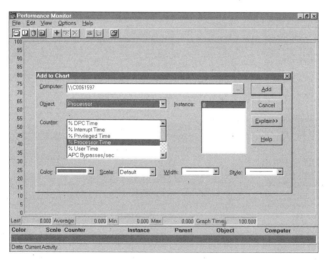

**Figure 7.7.** *Performance Monitor processor metrics*

Clicking on the metric in the counter scrolling window adds that metric to the display. You have the option of obtaining a description of a performance metric by clicking on the **Explain>>** button on the right. Other display attributes may also be selected at this time to uniquely identify this metric when it is plotted. Color, line width, and line style can all be chosen to make the metric easily identifiable.

Because the illustrations in this book are monochrome, line width is used to typify the chosen metrics. Figure 7.8 shows a Performance Monitor display listing what performance objects are available.

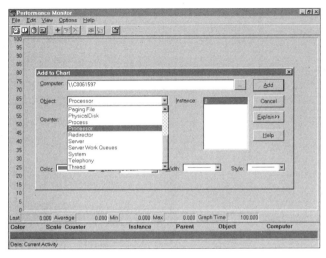

**Figure 7.8.** *Performance objects available to be measured*

Performance measurements can be observed for paging file activity, disk activity, thread operations, and much more. Figure 7.9 shows a graph of the percentage of time the CPU was busy, the percentage of time spent accommodating users, and how much processor time was spent processing interrupts.

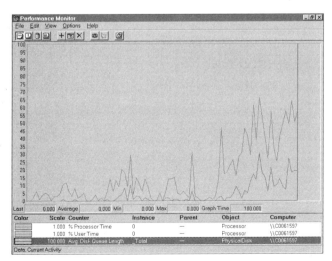

**Figure 7.9.** *A working Performance Monitor chart*

The long vertical line pointed to by the arrow moves once a second to the right, leaving a trail of performance data to the left. Once the vertical line reaches its farthest point to the right, it moves all the way to the left and starts painting the chart all over again.

Performance data can be logged to a disk file. This disk file data can be played back or used to produce a performance report. The data can also be exported into *.csv files and fed to a spreadsheet such as Microsoft Excel for further analysis.

# Appendix A

## References

### *Microsoft Windows*

*Inside the Windows NT File System*
by Helen Custer
Microsoft Press, September 1, 1994
ISBN: 155615660X

*Inside Windows*
by Bruce Hallberg, Forrest Houlette, and Jim Boyce
New Riders Pub., July 1, 1994
ISBN: 1562053280

*Inside Windows 95*
by Adrian King
Microsoft Press, October 1994
ISBN: 155615626X

*Inside Windows NT*
by Helen Custer
Microsoft Press, November 1, 1992
ISBN: 155615481X

*Inside Windows NT Workstation 4* (book and CD-ROM edition)
by Kathy Ivens, Bruce Hallberg, Bob Chronister, Drew Heywood,
    and George Eckel
New Riders Pub., October 1, 1996
ISBN: 1562056611

*Microsoft Windows 95 Resource Kit: The Technical Guide to*
   *Planning For, Installing, Configuring, and Supporting Windows*
   *95 in Your Organization* (book and disk edition)
by Microsoft Corporation
Microsoft Press, July 1, 1995
ISBN: 1556156782

*Programming Windows 95 (Microsoft Programming Series)*
by Charles Petzold
Microsoft Press, March 1, 1996
ISBN: 1556156766

*Programmer's Guide to Microsoft Windows 95: Key Topics on*
   *Programming for Windows from the Microsoft Windows*
   *Development Team*
by Microsoft Corporation
Microsoft Press, August 1995
ISBN: 1556158343

*Networking Windows NT 4.0: Workstation and Server — The Total*
   *Guide to Evaluating, Planning, Installing and Maintaining an*
   *NT Server Network*
by Martin Heller, David Methvin, Thomas Henderson, and
   John Ruley
John Wiley & Sons, January 1, 1997
ISBN: 0471175021

*Multithreaded Programming with Windows NT*
by Pankaj K. Garg and Thuan Pham
Prentice-Hall, December 1995
ISBN: 0131206435

*Win32 System Services: The Heart of Windows 95 and Windows NT,*
   2nd Edition
by Marshall Brain
Prentice-Hall, 1996
ISBN: 0133247325

## _Solaris_

_Solaris OpenWindows Deskset Reference/OpenWindows Version 3.1_
Prentice-Hall, February 1, 1993
ISBN: 0130357189

_Solaris System Administrator's Guide_
by Janet Winsor
Ziff Davis Press, October 1, 1992
ISBN: 1562760807

_Solaris Multithreaded Programming Guide_
Prentice-Hall, January 1995
ISBN: 0131608967

_Solaris 2.X: System Administrator's Guide_
by S. Lee Henry, John R. Graham, and Lee S. Henry
McGraw-Hill, October 1, 1994
ISBN: 0070293686

_Solaris_
by Stanislaw Lem
Harcourt Brace, June 1, 1987
ISBN: 0156837501

_Mastering Solaris 2_
by David F. Angell and Brent Heslop
Sybex, March 1, 1993
ISBN: 078211072X

_UNIX System Adminstration Handbook,_ 2nd Edition
by Evi Nemeth, Garth Snyder, Scott Seebass, and Trent R. Hein
Prentice-Hall, 1995
ISBN: 0131510517

## *Linux*

*Toolkit for Linux: Contains a Full Release of Linux in the Form of*
    *Slackware 2.0, for the More Experienced Linux Users/CDROM*
    *in Jewel Box*
Pub Group West, 1994
ISBN: 1571760644

*Slackware Linux Unleashed*
by Tim Parker and Kamran Husain
Sams, March 1, 1997
ISBN: 0672310120

*Linux Slackware 96: The Internet's Favorite 32-Bit Operating*
    *System*
Walnut Creek, July 1996
ISBN: 1571761500

*The Linux Database (Slackware Series)*
by Dorothy Forbes and Feed Butzen
MIS Press, March 1, 1997
ISBN: 1558284915

*Running Linux*
by Lar Kaufman and Matt Welsh
O'Reilly & Associates, August 1, 1996
ISBN: 1565921518

*Red Hat Linux Unleashed*
by Timothy Parker and Kamran Husain
Sams, June 1, 1996
ISBN: 0672309629

*Linux Programming (MIS Press Slackware Series)*
by Patrick Volkerding, Eric Foster-Johnson, and Kevin Reichard
M & T Books, January 1, 1997
ISBN: 1558285075

*Linux A to Z*
by Philip Cornes
Prentice-Hall, January 1, 1997
ISBN: 0137428677

*Special Edition Using Linux* (Slackware CD-ROM included)
by Jack Tackett, David Gunter, and Lance Brown
QUE, 1995
ISBN: 0789701006

# Appendix B

## Common User Commands

## UNIX

### Deleting a File

### OpenWindows File Manager

1. Drag file icon glyph to wastebasket
2. Select file glyph; select Delete from Edit menu

### Linux Command Line

```
rm -dfirv name...
```

| | |
|---|---|
| -d | Remove a directory even if directory is not empty |
| -f | Ignore nonexistent files and never prompt user |
| -i | Prompt user whether to remove file |
| -r | Remove directory contents recursively |
| -v | Print name of file before removing it |

### Solaris Command Line

```
rm -firps name...
```

| | |
|---|---|
| -f | Remove all files whether protected or not |
| -i | Prompt user whether to remove file |
| -r | Remove directory contents recursively |
| -p | Remove directory name and its parent directories |
| -s | Suppress messages to standard error when using -p |

### Renaming a File

### OpenWindows File Manager

Click SELECT on file name and display text field that can be edited

### Linux Command Line

```
mv -bfiuv source dest
```

-b     Make backups of files about to be removed

-f     Remove existing destination files and never prompt user

-i     Prompt user whether to overwrite each destination file

-u     Do not move a nondirectory file with same or newer destination time

-v     Print name of each file before moving it

### Solaris Command Line

```
mv -fi source dest
```

-f     Move files without prompting user

-i     Prompt user for move confirmation

### Copying a File

### OpenWindows File Manager

1. SELECT file or files to be copied; choose Cut or Copy from Edit menu; open folder to receive files, choose Paste from Edit menu
2. Drag and drop file glyph onto background of any open File Manager window or onto workspace

### Linux Command Line

```
cp -abdfilPprsuvx source dest
```

-a     Preserve as much attribute information as possible

-b     Make backups of files

-d     Copy symbolic links as symbolic links, preserve hard links

-f     Remove existing destination files

-i     Prompt user whether to overwrite existing destination file

-l      Link

-P      Form name of each destination file by appending to the target directory a slash and the specified source file name

-p      Preserve original file owner, group, permissions, and time stamps

-r      Copy directories recursively

-s      Make symbolic links instead of copies

-u      Do not update a nondirectory file that has an existing destination with same or newer modification time

-v      Print name of each file before copying it

-x      Skip subdirectories that are different file systems

## Solaris Command Line

```
cp [-fip] source_file target_file
```

-f      If file destination file descriptor cannot be obtained, unlink destination file

-i      Prompt user for copy confirmation

-p      Preserve all file attributes in the copy

## Creating a Directory

### OpenWindows File Manager

Select Create Folder from File menu

### Linux Command Line

```
mkdir -pm dir
```

-p      Ensure each given directory exists

-m      Set directory protection mode

### Solaris Command Line

```
mkdir -pm dir
```

-p      Ensure each given directory exists

-m      Set directory protection mode

### *Removing a Directory*

### *OpenWindows File Manager*

SELECT folder and choose DELETE from EDIT menu

### *Linux Command Line*

See `rm` command

### *Solaris Command Line*

See `rm` command

### *Changing File Permissions*

### *OpenWindows File Manager*

Select a file or group of files and click on Information from File menu

### *Linux Command Line*

```
chmod -Rcfv mode file ...
```

| | |
|---|---|
| `-R` | Change file permissions recursively |
| `-c` | Verbosely describe only files whose permissions actually change |
| `-f` | Do not print error messages about files whose permissions cannot be changed |
| `-v` | Verbosely describe changed permissions |

### *Solaris Command Line*

```
chmod -fR mode file ...
```

| | |
|---|---|
| `-f` | No complaints if change mode fails |
| `-R` | Recursively descend directory to perform change mode |

### *Get a Directory*

### *OpenWindows File Manager*

Select File Manager from Program menu

## *Linux Command Line*

```
ls -abcdefgimnopqrstuxABCFGLNQRSUX
```

-a    List all files, even dot files

-b    Quote nongraphic characters in file names

-c    Sort directory contents according to file status change time

-d    List directories like other files rather than their contents

-e    List file times in full

-f    Do not sort directory contents

-g    Ignored, needed for compatibility

-i    Print index number of each file

-m    List files horizontally, as many as will fit

-n    List numeric UID and GID instead of file name

-o    Colorize file name depending on type

-p    Append character to file name indicating file type

-q    Print question marks instead of nongraphic characters

-r    Sort directory in reverse order

-s    Print size of each file

-t    Sort directory by time stamp

-u    Sort directory according to files' last access time

-x    List files in columns sorted horizontally

-A    List all files except for '.' and '..'

-B    Do not list files that end with '~'

-C    List files in columns, sorted vertically

-F    Append character to file name indicating type

-G    Do not display group information

-L    List files linked to by symbolic links

-N    Do not quote file names

-Q    Enclose file names in quotes and quote nongraphic characters

-R    List file contents of all directories recursively

-S    Sort directory by file size instead of alphabetically

## Solaris Command Line

```
ls -aAbcCdfFgilLmnopqrRstux1
```

| | |
|---|---|
| -a | List all entries including those beginning with a "." |
| -A | Same as -a but do not list "." and ".." |
| -b | Force printing of nonprintable characters |
| -c | Use time of last modification for sorting |
| -C | Multicolumn output with entries sorted down the columns |
| -d | Do not list directory contents, just its name |
| -f | Force each argument to be intrerpreted as a directory |
| -F | Append character after file name to identify type |
| -g | Same as -l except owner is not displayed |
| -i | Print i-node number for each file displayed |
| -l | List file information in long format |
| -L | List file link reference rather than link itself |
| -m | List files across page separated by commas |
| -n | Same as -l except owner's UID and GID are printed |
| -o | Same as -l except that group is not printed |
| -p | Put a slash after each file name if file is a directory |
| -q | Force printing of nonprintable characters |
| -r | Sort file names in reverse order |
| -R | Recursively list subdirectories encountered |
| -s | Give size in blocks |
| -t | Sort by time stamp |
| -u | Use time of last access for sorting |
| -x | Multicolumn output with entries sorted across rather than down page |
| -1 | Print one entry per line of output |

## Sorting

### Linux Command Line

```
sort  [-cm] [-t separator] [-o output-file]
[-T tempdir] [-bdfiMnr] [+POS1 [-POS2]] [-k POS1[,POS2]]
   [file...]
```

-c      Check whether file is already sorted

-m      Merge files by sorting them as a group

### Solaris Command Line

```
sort [ -cm ] [ -o output ] [ -T directory ]
    [ -y [ kmem ]] [ -z recsz ] [ -dfiMnr ] [ - b  ]
    [- t char ][ -k keydef ] [ +pos1 [ -pos2 ]]
     [ file...]
```

-c      Check whether file is already sorted

-m      Merge files by sorting them as a group

## Compressing/Decompressing a File (Creating a .Z File)

### Linux and Solaris Command Line

```
compress [-cfv] [-b bits] [file]

uncompress [-cfv] [ file...]

zcat [ file...]
```

# Microsoft Windows

## Deleting a File

### Explorer

1. Drag file icon to wastebasket
2. Right-click on folder/file name and select Delete

### MS-DOS Window

```
DELETE filename
```

### *Renaming a File*

### *Explorer*

Right-click on folder/file name and select Rename, then enter new name

### *MS-DOS Window*

```
RENAME old-name new-name
```

### *Copying a File*

### *Explorer*

1. Click on file/folder to be copied
2. In Edit menu, click on Copy
3. Create/open file/folder to copy to
4. In Edit menu, click on Paste

### *MS-DOS Window*

```
COPY from-file to-file
```

### *Changing File Permissions/Properties ....*

### *Explorer (NT only)*

Right-click on file/folder name and select Properties to change file owership

### *Explorer (Windows 95)*

Right-click on file/folder name and select Properties to change file attributes (read-only, archive, system, hidden)

### *MS-DOS Window*

```
ATTRIB [option] filename
```

## *Compressing/Decompressing Files*

### *Explorer*

Install WINZip

### *MS-DOS Window*

Use public-domain pkzip/pkunzip utilities

## *Sorting Files*

### *Explorer*

Click button panels above file viewing window; can sort files by name, type, size, and modification time by clicking the appropriate button panel

### *MS-DOS Window*

```
sort /R /+n input-file output-file
```

| | |
|---|---|
| /R | Sort in reverse order |
| /+n | Sort starting at $n$th position |

# Appendix C

# Windows Tasks and Keyboard Shortcuts

## *Windows Tasks and Keyboard Shortcuts*

| *Task* | *Shortcut* |
|---|---|
| Open the **Start** menu | **Ctrl+Esc** |
| Minimize all windows | **Alt+M** (taskbar selected) |
| Quit current program | **Alt+F4** |
| Put active window onto Clipboard | **Alt+Print Screen** |
| Reduce window | **Alt+Spacebar+R** |
| Enlarge window | **Alt+Spacebar+X** |
| Minimize active window | **Alt+Spacebar+N** |
| Control menu | **Alt+Spacebar** |
| Help | **F1** |
| Go to end of document | **Ctrl+End** |
| Go to beginning of document | **Ctrl+Home** |
| Bypass CD autorun | **Shift** during insert |
| Delete without putting into recycle bin | **Shift+Delete** on selected object |
| Select all folders in Explorer | **Ctrl+A** |
| Find a folder in Explorer | **F3** |
| Go to folder in Explorer | **Ctrl+G** |
| Go to parent folder in Explorer | **Backspace** |
| Undo | **Ctrl+Z** |

| *Task* | *Shortcut* |
|---|---|
| Toggle StickyKeys on/off | Tap **Shift** 5 times |
| Toggle FilterKeys on/off | Hold down **Right Shift** for 8 seconds |
| Turn ToggleKeys on/off | Hold down **Num Lock** for 5 seconds |
| Toggle MouseKeys on/off | **Left Alt+Left Shift+Num Lock** |
| Display context menu for selected item | **Shift+F10** |
| Rename selected file | **F2** |
| Place file into the recycle bin | **Delete** |
| Switch DOS window between full screen and window | **Alt+Enter** |

# Appendix D

## Enhancing System Performance

T he key to streamlining system operation is to activate the **Control Panel** and double-click on the **System** icon to get the **System Properties** window, as depicted in Figure D.1.

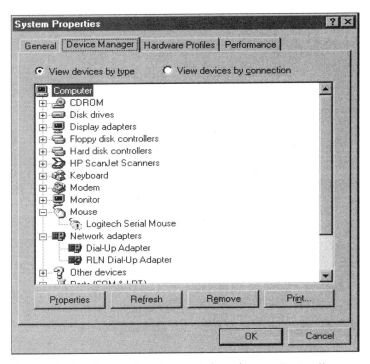

**Figure D.1.** *System Properties window showing Device Manager contents*

The **System Properties** window is where you can establish settings affecting the performance of your system. The two important tabs in this window are **Device Manager** and **Performance**. The **Device**

**Manager** tab has been selected in Figure D.1 and gives a visual list of all the devices connected to this computer. By clicking on the expansion button, you can obtain more detailed information about a particular device. Once you click on a device listed in the window, you can select any of the buttons listed at the bottom of the window to perform more device-management tasks, such as removing the device or adjusting its properties. If communication to a device fails, a red X is displayed over the device icon. The **Performance** tab produces the window depicted in Figure D.2.

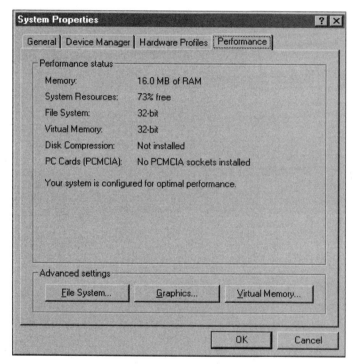

**Figure D.2.** *System Properties Performance tab display*

The **Performance** tab allows settings for the file system, the graphics environment and memory management. This window plays a crucial role in optimizing these configurations. Clicking on **Graphics...** produces the window in Figure D.3. This window controls how aggressively Windows will pursue using your video adapter hardware features, specifically the graphics accelerator. The more sophisticated graphics available today function ideally when the slider is set to full.

Sometimes, however, visually intensive applications may hang, and it may be necessary to adjust the setting of the accelerator use slider.

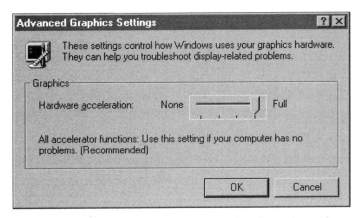

**Figure D.3.** *The advanced graphics window from the Performance tab of the System Properties window*

The **File System...** tab produces the window seen in Figure D.4. This window allows settings for the hard drive and CD-ROM. The settings are related to cache sizes. Depending on how you use your system, it may be possible to improve memory availability by reducing the size of some of these caches. The CD-ROM tab produces the window shown in Figure D.5.

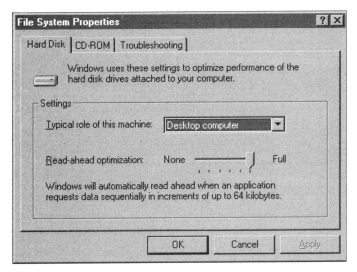

**Figure D.4.** *The File Systems Properties window from the Performance tab of the System Properties window*

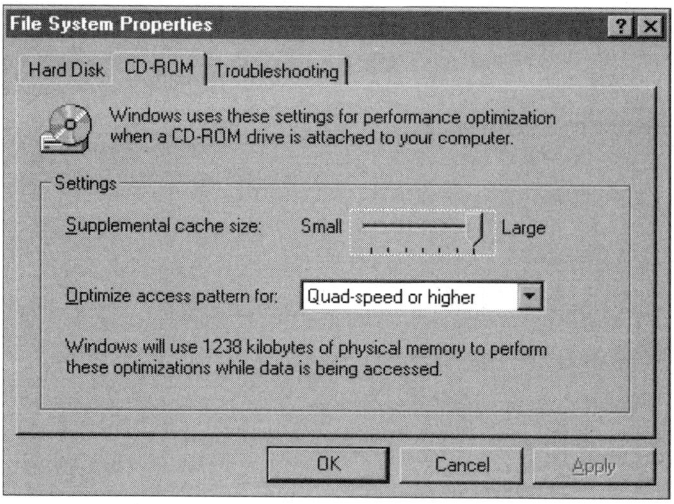

**Figure D.5.** *File System Properties window for the CD-ROM*

Here you have the opportunity to adjust for the type of CD-ROM that is installed on your system. The CD-ROM settings should be based on how you use your system. If you run intensive multimedia applications, you need to set the cache setting high, however, some users just use the CD-ROM to install software and do not require as extensive a cache allocation.

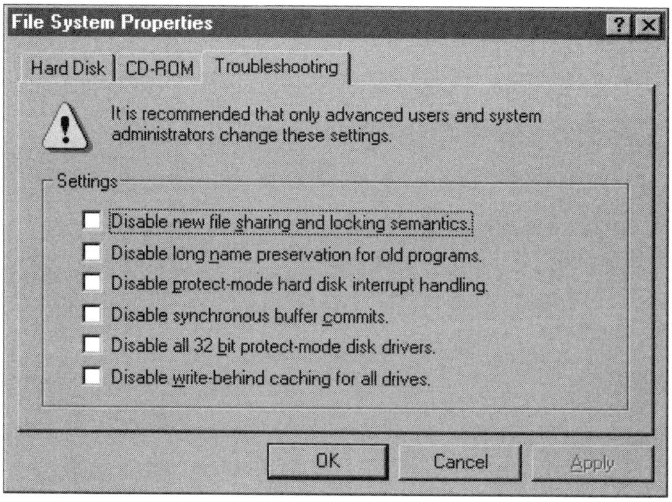

**Figure D.6.** *The Troubleshooting window from File System Properties*

The **Troubleshooting** tab should be used with caution. The features that are controlled from this tab can have a major system-wide impact. Figure D.6 illustrates the contents of the **Troubleshooting** tab. Caution is urged because selecting any of the items listed will degrade Windows performance.

The last tab to mention is **Virtual Memory** which gives the user the option of specifying the location and size of virtual memory. Figure D.7 depicts the **Virtual Memory** tab window.

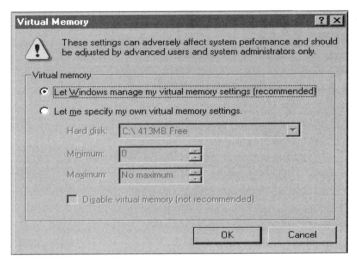

**Figure D.7.** *The Virtual Memory tab from the System Properties window*

# Appendix E

## Using the Registry

### Preserving the Registry

A backup copy of the registry should always be maintained if you are going to be manipulating entries in it. A corrupted registry can severely compromise the successful operation of your system. However, careful use of the registry allows you unparalleled control over your Windows environment. A multitude of environmental characteristics can be controlled through the registry that are unattainable to the ordinary user. The Win95 CD contains a registry backup utility CFGBACK.EXE which can be found in the OTHER\MISC\CFGBACK folder. CFGBACK.EXE should be copied to your desktop for easy access.

### How to Manipulate Registry Entries

The registry is manipulated with the Registry Editor (REGEDIT) which can be initiated from the **Start** box, selecting **Run** and then entering REGEDIT. Figure E.1 illustrates the initial REGEDIT screen.

**Figure E.1.** *Initial Registry Editor screen*

The Registry Editor is an extraordinary facility once you realize the scope of the registry itself. Attempting to edit the register by any other means would be impossible. Because of the hierarchical relationship of the registry entries, the ability to point and click your way to the various entries ensures that the correct information is accessed. Figure E.2 illustrates the extensive makeup of the registry.

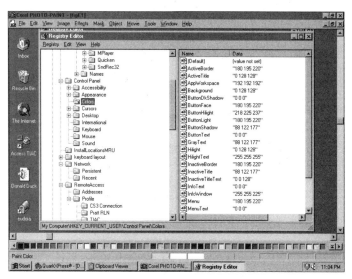

**Figure E.2.** *Example of scope of registry data*

The *Microsoft Windows Resource Kits* are the official source about registry entries. Serious registry editor users should keep these references handy.

### How to Eliminate the Recycle Bin

In the Registry Editor, go to the following path:

```
HKEY_LOCAL_MACHINE\SOFTWARE\Microsoft\Windows\CurrentVersion\
    explorer\Desktop\NameSpace
```

Keep clicking on each of the character strings until **Recycle Bin** is found in the right pane. Hitting the **Delete** key eliminates the **Recycle Bin**.

### *How to Preserve Your Desktop Layout*

1. From the Registry Editor, find this path:

```
HKEY_CURRENT_USER\SOftware\Microsoft\Windows\CurrentVersion\
    Polices\Explorer
```

2. Go to the right pane and select **New/DWORD**

3. Rename value **NoSaveSettings** and hit the **Enter** key

4. Right-click on new **NoSaveSettings** and select **Modify**

5. Enter the number 1 in the **Value** data box

6. Click on **OK** and exit

### *How to Speed Up the Start Menus*

1. From the Registry Editor, find this path:

```
HKEY_CURRENT_USER\Control Panel\Desktop
```

2. In the right pane, right-click on white space and select **New\String Value**
3. Enter **MenuShowDelay** as new value and hit the **Enter** key
4. Double-click on **MenuShowDelay** and enter a number from 1 to 10; the lower the number, the faster the menus cascade

### *How to Make Your BMP Images Appear in Explorer as Icon Versions of Themselves*

1. From the Registry Editor, find this path:

```
HKEY_CLASSES_ROOT/Paint.Picture/DefaultIcon
```

2. Double-click on the right pane and modify value of **DefaultIcon** to %1

# Index